Live in Love
A Life Handbook
for the New Golden Age

by Mikaelah Cordeo, Ph.D.
Messages from
Mother - Father God
and Lord Jesus the Cosmic Christ

Live in Love - A Life Handbook for the New Golden Age
3rd edition, copyright © 2013 by Mikaelah Cordeo, Ph.D.
First published as *Love Will Steer the Stars* in 2000. Now updated and
expanded.

Passage from *A Course in Miracles*, copyright 1975, 1992, 1999,
reprinted by permission of the Foundation for *A Course in Miracles*, Inc.
- Roscoe, NY 12776.

Passage from *Initiation, Human and Solar* by Alice A. Bailey,
Lucis Publishing Company reprinted by permission of Lucis Trust,
which holds the copyright.

ISBN: 978-0-9827818-0-7
For permissions, condensations, translations or adaptations, write the
publisher at the address below.

Published by:
Golden Rose Publishing
P.O. Box 810
Mount Shasta. CA 96067
email: mcordeo1@gmail.com
Webpage: http://www.mcordeo.4t.com

Printed in the United States of America

by Mikaelah Cordeo, Ph.D.   • iii

Blessings

11-11-08

This book is our gift to Ascending humanity. We have imbued it not just with our Love and Blessings but with hundreds of seed thoughts to inspire each of you to explore, to express, and to inspire in your turn.

Our wish for you is that you might be the fertile ground on which our seeds are sown and that a great harvest might be reaped by each of you—a harvest of Love, of understanding, of grace and of true wealth.

Our blessings are with you always.

Mother/Father God

Health and Wealth and Blessings of the One Who is the All. We love you and we greet you. We are the Elohim

We wish to also extend our Love and Blessings to each of you. We have each and all blessed and infused this book with Love and Wisdom and Power.

This is a time of tremendous growth and expansion for the people of Earth. Do not be dismayed by the changes you see around you. Rather, give thanks that there is a renewal blazing across the Earth. Give thanks for the hundreds and thousands of blessings you each receive every day. And give thanks that God/Goddess is in full command of spaceship Earth.

And all of you – each one of you – is now receiving every blessing and inspiration to live your life to the highest and the best that human hearts can aspire.

Only that which comes from Love will remain on Earth. That is our blessing and our gift to you

Give thanks, for it is so done!

We are the Elohim

Awakening to the New Golden Age

12-21-2012

Beloved Ones,

We are the Elohim and we greet you in the name of All That Is. We wish to extend our welcome to all on Earth at this time, as we now officially enter the New Golden Age. This is a time of tremendous creativity and transformation. All that has gone before is but a fraction of that which is to come. Because all that has gone before was within the structure and the expectation of all that you know as the third dimension. The miracles of creation in the fifth dimension will be unfolding for you daily.

You may know us as the creators of Universes. It is a wondrous part of the unfolding Divine Plan that Earth hold a new field of consciousness that enables all to be unified with their own I Am Presence — the Indiviudality of God. Additionally it is a time of soul groups re-uniting and working within the unified collective I Am. It is the time of the fullness of your blended Self — human and Divine — to fully express the great God gifts of this incarnation. Your greatest hopes and dreams will be fullfilled. It is the time of your co-creation of the Earth and her role in the ongoing creative expansion of the Universe.

Earth herself will be working with you in this process. We invite you to see one another as God in form. Allow yourself to know and to rejoice in the fulfillment of your Divine Plan and Purpose with full support in every way. And we delight with you in the vision becoming reality of Heaven on Earth.

May you be bathed in every Heavenly Grace during this transition phase.

We are the Elohim

Table of Contents

List of Exercises

Chapter One

The Rebirth of
the Age of the Mother

Mother God Speaks:

Beloved Ones,

I am your Divine Mother.

I am One with All that Is.

I speak to you now after Eons of Silence—because it is now time for the Rebirth of the Age of the Mother.

We ask that you come with us on a journey—a journey of transformation, a journey of transfiguration—as we look at your recent history.

The year is 1987. Look for a moment at the Earth from the perspective of your astronauts. You see it as beautiful, glowing, a jewel in the heavens, white clouds gently swirl across a blue-green world.

Then as you draw nearer, you begin to see layers of pollution in the atmosphere. Signs of damage include clear cutting in the rain forests and urban sprawl under thick layers of murk. Closer still you can hear the sounds of chaos across the planet. Cars in gridlock, horns blaring. In extreme cases enraged drivers go berserk, harming themselves or others.

Many teens are lost and abandoned, roaming the city streets, both stalker and prey. No social moral fiber sustains their agonized searching. Drugs and urban decay rot the cities. Poverty drags people into hopelessness and despair.

Working people struggle to keep up with endless bills. In Third World countries, revolt, revenge and war crush human values and destroy lives and property.

The oceans are dying; the waterways are polluted with chemicals, urban refuse and acid rain. Whales and dolphins are sacrificial victims of a world gone mad. The indigenous peoples live lives of alcoholism, poverty and despair. Their cultures are a tattered remnant of the past, their lives often soaked in alcohol to deaden the pain of tragedy upon tragedy, loss upon loss.

> *A doorway appeared through which*
> *streamed a Light that triggered*
> *the hearts and minds*
> *of those who had come*
> *with one purpose to planet Earth.*

Into this land of beauty and destruction, rich and poor, mechanical marvels and chaos, came a Ray of Light. On August 16 and 17, 1987, a Ray of Light reached the Earth from the Galactic Sun. Vast starry alignments had shifted across the heavens until—in that moment of Cosmic Time—a doorway appeared through which streamed a Light that triggered the hearts and minds of those who had come with one purpose to planet Earth. They had come to participate in the collective rebirth of this precious jewel. Each knew full well the traumas and the dramas that would await them. They each had agreed to clear planetary and cosmic karma, in addition to any personal soul (karmic) lessons that were needed.

It is said that this is the Cosmic Day of Courage. (One Cosmic day is many thousands of your Earth years.) Each of these souls drank deeply of Courage and Faith before their emergence here.

Each would be tested full measure in Courage and Faith throughout their lives. They committed themselves wholeheartedly to the risks of entry into Earth embodiment.

*These souls drank deeply
of Courage and Faith
before their emergence here.*

Take a moment here and see yourself—the long preparation, the goal of world service shining in your eyes, the fire of love and dedication filling your hearts, the last instructions, the last Breath of Life filling your soul in Perfection's alignment, then a swift sense of diving deeper and deeper to emerge—in an infant's body. The journey begins.

You have each had your traumas and your dramas. Stand here with me for another moment watching all unfold.

***

Let that Eternal Watcher send to you now a new Cup filled with Divine Grace. Drink deeply and quench your thirst until the Cup is empty. Allow that Grace to heal your wounds, to soothe your tortured heart, to refill your measure of Courage, to bring back full remembrance of your goal.

Breathe it in and allow yourself to just Be with it for a moment

***

The Light touched each of you and it touched the collective soul, the heart of Mother Earth, and triggered a Great Awakening.

Many of you had already begun this awakening process. Each of you had an inner timing built in. Based on life events, you were moving forward to take your place in the new drama that was unfolding within and around you.

Those who awakened early helped to build the foundations on which those who came later would stand and stretch and grow and build. These in turn built the next stage from which others would launch themselves.

A great endeavor was launched; and each individual carried a piece of the Plan.

Many were awed to find kindred souls awakening to the same dreams half a world away. Without a clear organizational structure that third dimensional eyes could see, the Light workers began to awaken and take up their appointed tasks. There would have been massive resistance had there been a clear organizational unit, but there was nothing visible to attack. Each seemed to be an independent unit. Their ideas seemed strange but no threat because they touched so few.

Yet those few awakened and touched others, and still there was nothing obvious to create resistance. No one thing said, "yes, this is the New Age Movement." There was obviously something. You felt it when you met one another and recognized your shared purpose. You came together in celebration and unity for December 31st World Peace meditations, full moons, 11:11's, Wesak's and Galactic events that filled your hearts and minds. Doorways opened, you joined together, stepped through, and the patterns dissolved to be re-formed in new groups, new events. Still, no structure emerged and yet tremendous growth was happening across the planet.

See these patterns now as if they were some vast biochemical event. The molecules swirl and touch, the chemical bonds are formed, new compounds are created—then light and heat are applied—the bonds are broken again, and the process repeats itself at the next level.

This is what has been happening. The vast structure that is emerging is coming into being through the transformation of you as individuals. The bonds that hold together this emerging Being—this collective Presence—are the bonds of Love.

You are exploring what you love, whom you love, how you love. What is love? How do you love yourself, one another, the Earth?

As you look at your lives, you begin to see how Love calls you forward out of patterns that no longer serve you, through trials and tribulations, yes—but ever forward into greater joy, greater wisdom, greater respect for yourself and all Life.

You begin to see how
Love calls you forward.

For Love is the Light that is touching the Earth and all people and creatures upon her. Your eyes are opening. Daily, you are choosing to turn from fear and anger and ugliness to joy and nurturing and beauty.

In 1996, it was announced that the Earth had ascended. In her article, A Time for Clarity and Understanding, 1997, spiritual author and teacher Patricia Cota Robles reported: "We completed our Ascension into the Fourth Dimension on August 22, 1996. Now we are hurtling at warp speed toward the initial impulse of our Ascension on the Fifth Dimensional Spiral of Evolution."

And from Lord Sunanda in 1997:

Planetary Ascension

(Excerpt from Message from Lord Sunanda through Mikaelah Cordeo in the Spring, 1997, issue of the newsletter 'Starfire Vision.')

"And we wish to acknowledge all of you. Each and every one of you has been significant in the accomplishment of our goal. The Earth has ascended! The Earth has reached that state that you/we have all worked for these millennia. It may not seem outrageously different here to you, however, we assure you that it is so. Well then, if you can't see it or feel it, what exactly does it mean?

It means that those life streams that formerly were separated from the Light and Love of their Beloved I Am Presence* are now able to know and experience the Love that desires to be Known. It means that more than 50 % of the life streams of Earth have chosen the way of Love.

As they are lifted up, they in turn lift up those who have not yet chosen. Their energy field, their love and service assist others.

We are anticipating that there will continue to be appreciable differences in the ways in which life is lived here on Earth. There are already many trends to which we can point. You will continue to see an acceleration of the ways of love and a deceleration and dispersing of the ways of fear."

More than one-half of the people of Earth have chosen Love. This is a tremendous achievement. Success pulled from the brink of nuclear disaster.

Two thousand years ago, Jesus Christ created a Divine Template—a perfect model—of Love in action. For two thousand years we have been slowly absorbing what that would mean for us as individuals and for us collectively.

A church emerged, teachings developed and were shared. Disputes arose, distortions abounded and still the Template held. Century after century, Love and Truth were the bedrock.

We still stand on that foundation as the New Age emerges. We are washing away the distortions and confusions from

---

*I Am Presence - This name designates the Individualized expression of Mother/Father God consciousness, also known as the oversoul and Higher Self. As one moves into higher and higher levels of consciousness, one integrates more and more of this Presence with the human personality self. Eventually all sense of separation is gone. You know: "I and the Father are One." "I and the Mother are One."

individual and collective psyches. As clarity grows, so does the stability of what is being built.

Love is the foundation of what is emerging. Love is the mortar that holds the bricks of our new structures together. Love will fill our lives with grace and meaning as we step forward into the new.

> *Love is the foundation*
> *of what is emerging.*

The old structures were rigid, and so, when someone or something came forward that threatened to change them, it meant the annihilation of what had been. It is no wonder that people reacted so violently to change agents. Their whole lives were threatened.

The new framework is flexible, growth-oriented. Change is incorporated easily and naturally. The unusual has its opportunity to grow and develop in harmony with the whole. The change agents and the prophets can be revered and respected, not silenced and killed. That which is natural and serves the whole can grow in safety.

Lord Jesus the Cosmic Christ takes up the story:

Beloved Ones in Christ, I am with you now and always. Did I not say unto you, "I shall be with you, even unto the end of the world" (Matthew 28:20).

In this chapter, which is offering an overview of the last few years since 1987, I would like to speak of My Emergence into form which has accelerated since that time. Indeed, as the consciousness of humanity has been raising itself in response to the Light flooding the Earth, I have been more fully able to unite with and express through many of you.

You have awaited My Coming on a Cloud of Glory—and perhaps I shall. Once I was awaited as a mighty king to destroy My people's enemies. I came instead as a simple Babe in a manger.

But the Bible equally speaks of seeing Me in your fellow men and women. This is not just a pious thought, a metaphor or abstract concept. Of those whose hearts and minds are truly filled with the Light and Love of God—the Holy Spirit—I Am fully One with them.

You may know those who have been shining lights unto the world on a grand scale and say, "Oh, yes, well maybe St. Francis, St. Thérèse of Lisieux, or Mother Theresa in modern times." Or stretching yourselves, you might even see me in Gandhi or Albert Schweitzer. But I say unto you, there are *many* more whose bodies and souls are flesh of my flesh—fully One with me.

It could be your gentle and generous neighbor or the delightful and outrageous friend who always makes you laugh and who seems able to wring every ounce of enjoyment from her life.

Perhaps you know someone who loves flowers and tends them so that all may share their beauty or an older friend who remembers everyone on their birthdays and special occasions.

With some, I am fully merged, ever present, though sometimes in the background, sometimes speaking words of love and comfort to friends and neighbors, offering a gentle touch or quiet help. With others, and there are many, it is a more temporary alignment—but no less real. And lives are touched by my Presence again. For is there not a longing across this planet in the hearts and minds of those who know of me—to truly know me, to see me as I move about my daily tasks? Some of you ask yourselves, "What would Jesus do in a case like this? What would He be like today in jeans and a T-shirt working on my car, in a tuxedo telling jokes at a fund-raising event, or writing songs to lift the heart?"

There are millions who have longed to see me, and who

truly have, but didn't quite know it or believe it. I say to you, ask in your hearts if I have ever come to you in this way. If you have not yet had this experience, ask to have it soon and to have a sign that it was truly me. Ask God for the eyes to see me in your neighbor or a passing stranger, and begin to understand the qualities of Life and Joy and Appreciation and Love I bring to this world. Begin to understand how easily you can do the same.

For those of you who love me, know that I will come to you and live in you and be One with you, if that is the longing of your heart. There is no need for thoughts of unworthiness or "not good enough." Many have prayed:

> *"O Lord I am not worthy*
> *that Thou should come to me,*
> *but speak the words of comfort,*
> *my spirit healed shall be."*

This was intended to foster a spirit of humility, but it does not serve you or me to think or pray in this way, if it keeps us apart.

I long to be with you—as you long to be with me. Hold no barriers between us. Not humility, nor feelings of unworthiness, nor grandiose ideas of the great deeds and miracles you will do.

It is Love that calls me to you: Love of you for me and me for you; Love of you for your husband or wife or child or mother or father. I am there when there is Love. You can call me to be with you when you desire more and greater Love to flow in your family, in your work, in the activities of the world

It is Love that calls me to you.

From *A Course in Miracles* comes this new prayer which I encourage you to use if you feel the desire to relate to God in a spirit of self-esteem.

"I who am Host to God am worthy of Him.
He who established His dwelling place in me,
created it as He would have it be.
It is not needful that I make it ready for Him,
But only that I do not interfere with His plan
*to restore to me my own awareness of
my readiness, which is eternal.
I need add nothing to His plan.
But to receive it, I must be willing not to
substitute my own in place of it."*
A Course in Miracles. (text, p. 356)

Beloved Ones, I would speak to you of channeling for a moment here. Most of you have heard of it. Many of you have experienced it "officially," that is, from one who clearly says "I am a channel for so and so." Many more of you have experienced it unofficially through inspired ministers, friends or yourselves in moments of Grace. Perhaps in a difficult situation you said, "Lord, help me find the right words to comfort this beloved friend," and I did.

What I wish for you to understand now is that in this way some of you have been preparing yourself to become a vehicle for my Light. Now some might say, "But I channel George or Bill or Mother Mary or St. Germain," and yet I say to you, if it comes in Love, it comes from God. For, while I came to you once as Jesus Christ, I now come to you through/ as Mary, Bill, George or St. Germain. For, I Am the Spirit of Love which permeates all things. I Am forever One with God/Goddess/All that Is—and beyond that as well.

Receiving these expressions of Love and Light within your physical bodies helps to transform you from your atomic structure on up. As your cells grow accustomed to greater and greater levels of Light, you become a living vehicle for the Light, one that is capable of transmitting greater and greater levels of Light. Eventually you are transformed into living Light—Temples of the Holy Spirit.

It is the Divine Plan that God express through humanity, both individually and collectively. Many have experienced this Divine integration. Channeling is only one way. There are many others. Each will find their own perfect way.

It is the Divine Plan that God express through humanity.

Some of you are finding yourselves uniting with aspects of God that you never expected. Certainly those of you who are beginning to have the experience of seeing God expressed in your friends and neighbors never expected this.

There are those who have been given the gift of discerning spirits (one of the gifts of the Holy Spirit mentioned by Paul in 1 Cor:12-14). These have seen the Angelic presence of Archangel Michael in one, Mother Mary in others, Beloved Jesus in still others.

If this is your experience, you are not crazy nor suffering from delusions of grandeur. Of course, it does take some emotional and psychological healing not to get carried away with what is happening. If you do get off track though, the Presence will withdraw until you once again align with Love.

There are those who have seen Lord Maitreya, Gautama Buddha, Shiva, Krishna, Isis and Quan Yin expressed not just in one or two individuals, but in many. Now, as this is happening and we are seeing it, we then have to say, what does it mean? This book is not going to explore that particular topic in depth; however, it is happening and we do have an opportunity to say we are worthy of uniting with these Divine Beings.

A recent movie, *Little Buddha*, explored this idea of multiple incarnations. It tells a true story of the search for a reincarnate Tibetan lama, a Rinpoche. This particular lama was a very high teacher, indeed, and recognized as a reincarnation of the Buddha. In the surprise ending, all three of the children that are being tested are identified as aspects of the same being reborn.

In the *Bhagavad-Gita*, Lord Krishna was said to be in over 10,000 separate bodies simultaneously during his lifetime. There is still much to understand here, but one thing is clearly emerging. It is the Divine Plan that God unite with us in form. In order for this to happen we must align more and more with Love and heal all that is within us that is not that Love.

ഇ

Author's comment: What does it mean to see God in your neighbors and your friends? For one thing, it means that Love has an awful lot of flavors. What does it mean that God might be in you? It means that God loves you a lot. It means that God/Goddess doesn't experience separation from you.

In the thirties, Alice Bailey channeled a book called "The Reappearance of the Christ and the Masters of Wisdom." I don't think anyone expected it to look like what we are now experiencing.

In the early part of this century, Krishnamurti was recognized as a young boy to be the one who would hold the Presence of Lord Maitreya (the Buddha who is to come, and in esoteric understanding, the Cosmic Christ for the Earth, the World Teacher). Many thought that he rejected this role and that it didn't happen.

He had been prepared for many years to take on this role. In one very dramatic moment, he stood before a large group assembled to hear him and told them that God was within each of them and not to look to him, particularly. He then left the organization and took up his role of teacher from a vastly different position than anyone had expected.

For those familiar with his life, it is clear that he really was a vehicle for Lord Maitreya. Humanity just didn't really know what to expect or how it would look. We still don't, but there is learning by living in these times.

Perhaps you want to know how exactly you recognize such a one. Is it because they are tall or good looking or have a fiery countenance? Is it red hair, or a high degree from college, great wealth or being a teacher, a monk or a doctor? All of these are externals and while they are often the reflection of high spiritual advancement, they are not necessary at all.

There are two qualities that will be the factors to help you identify such a one. One is the quality of Love and sheer goodness that is expressed. The more you love others, the better you will be able to see it in them. The second quality is from the faculty of Wisdom. These ones will speak words of wisdom, comfort and be of great assistance to those with the "ears to hear."

When you feel that a particular person is an Angel, because somehow "they look like an Angel," allow yourself to trust that you aren't crazy or misguided. In our difficult third dimensional world, you don't find these ones to be perfect. Even Jesus said, "Why callest thou me good? [there is] none good but one, [that is] God: but if thou wilt enter into life, keep the commandments." (Matthew 19:17).

What you may find is that you are called to be a little better, a little nicer, a bit more loving because of being with them and coming to know them. You might be called to look at yourself and set your standards a little higher.

Do you wonder if Jesus and Lord Maitreya are in some kind of a competition to see who is the best Christ? Does one negate the other? Does one invalidate the truth of the other?

It has been my privilege to experience the Presences of both Lord Jesus and Lord Maitreya. I can honestly tell you that the amount of Love that they both express does not lend itself to comparison. Neither of them would consider it appropriate to even comment on who is more important or bigger or better.

Love does not work that way. It is an opportunity to learn that Love is greater and more diverse than we ever dreamed. I always thought that Shiva, the Destroyer, would not be that fun to meet. But I have seen one of his chosen bodies. I have seldom seen that much love coming out of another human being. So, I have had to rethink my ideas about Shiva and about Hinduism.

What has all this meant to me as a Christian? Christ told us to love one another, and he didn't say anything about only others who believe the same way we do. So I am learning to love the Divine expressions of other religions. I don't think it makes me less a Christian. I think it makes me a better one. For myself it has been a lesson in God that is beyond anything I ever knew to dream of or ask for.

൭൩

Lord Jesus continues:

This beloved channel once had a conversation with God. It went something like this.

MC: (Following a distinct feeling that God was not pleased when I was thinking that God and Christ were not the same, I said:) "But, God, I have felt the Presence of Christ and I have felt Your Presence. They don't feel exactly the same. I'm sorry, but I don't get it. How are you the same?"

She heard this answer:

"If God is the ocean, the Christ is the wetness,"

and she understood—the Christ, the Love, permeates all things. It is not the only quality of God. Just as the ocean is also salty, filled with fish, plants, rocks, and so on. Wetness is an essential element of every drop of the ocean, and Love is an essential element of every part of All that Is.

There is, of course, vastly more to God than the ocean and yet as a metaphor it makes its point; and my point to you is: I Am the Love and I live in you. The depth and height and breadth of Love that I can be in you is up to you.

If you love Buddha, I am in the Buddha. If you love Mother Mary, I am in Mother Mary. If you love the Goddess, Shiva, Krishna, Quan Yin, Sai Baba, or Mother Meera, I am there as well.

I Am the Love and I live in you.

If your experience of Christianity was one filled with hypocrisy, or all show and no substance, know that who I Am, what I Am, is Love. Wherever you find that Love, there I Am. Forgive any and all who might have tainted your experience of Me, and allow my Love to fill you. For all Love is My Love.

If Christianity serves you to know My Love, then continue to grow and expand in that framework. If another religion or none at all serves you better to grow in Love, then trust your own knowingness. Trust your heart to know the Way, the Truth and the Life. For, humans make mistakes in their learning and growing, and human organizations reflect those mistakes sometimes. Some churches in their zeal to protect the ignorant and the innocent from mistakes have used fear to keep their congregations 'safe'. I ask that this stop now! Fear is not My tool. The ends do not justify the means.

Search your hearts. Root out that which is not from Me. Words of judgment, condemnation and hatred have no place in churches which claim to honor me.

If your church is focusing their energies in this way, vote with your feet. Do not argue or attempt to persuade anyone who does not wish to hear, but know you this: these are the end times. By your choices, conscious or unconscious, you are choosing Me or rejecting Me.

More than one-half of the population of this planet has chosen Love. This is a major factor in the transformation of thought and life that is underway at this time. It is the major factor that has kept the Earth changes from being worse than they have been.

Earth has ascended in consciousness to an alignment with the energies of Love—of the Christ. Those who cannot stay in harmony with this will self-select their own right place. For now, there are still wars, famine, poverty, and crime. There is still hatred, bigotry, revenge, criticism and condemnation. Those who choose these experiences will gravitate to their own hells. Those who choose love will be drawn—guided by the Angels—into their own heavens. Heaven is truly a state of mind.

Soon, there will be nothing left on Earth of the darker choices. Many of you are experiencing Heaven on Earth now because that is where you place your attention. Your hearts and minds are filled with Joy, Peace, Brotherhood, Love and Gratitude. There is little or no room for other experiences.

Heaven is truly a state of mind. Pay attention to where your thoughts dwell. Allow yourself to choose the life you desire. It is God's Will for you that you live in Heaven. It is indeed God's Will that Heaven and Earth be One

It is God's Will that
Heaven and Earth be One.

Author's Note: As time passes, we gain an even deeper understanding of the messages we receive. In terms of Planetary Ascension, the planet has indeed shifted to the 4th Dimension and is moving steadily into full alignment with the 5th Dimension. Each dimensional shift will also incorporate another planetary Ascension.

Furthermore, as of 2001, the entire Solar System took an Ascension Initiation, and the physical, emotional, mental and spiritual changes on Earth continue to accelerate.

For many there has been the desire to take a rest from the constant attention on healing and clearing of negativity. It is not yet time to rest. The forces of the anti-Christ are not resting and neither can we. When your attention is called to the negativity of the outer world, spend no time in anger or recrimination. Rather, go within and clear, clear, clear yet again, all that is reflected to you in the mirror of the world

The greater our advancement, the deeper we must go in our transformation. Our progress is enormous, but continue on until we reach our goal of bringing all along with us on this journey into Bliss.

The Tribulation Begins

In January of 2001, I was advised in several ways that the Earth had entered the official seven years of the Tribulation as prophesied in the book of Revelations in the Bible. Many books came my way to give me clarity about this, including "Flight of the Phoenix" by Mary Summer Rain with prophecies by her teacher No Eyes in which there were some remarkable correlations to the political events that surrounded George Bush's stepping into the Presidency of the United States of America. In this book, Mary asked, "Can't these prophecies be changed? What if we have a different president?" Her teacher told her, "No, it might be delayed, but they will happen."

It is my personal interpretation that the Clinton years represented that delay. As well, I felt at the time that we entered a distinctly different probability track then. While we have returned to the earlier track, the eight years in this alternate field has changed us all. We have the memories of what that kind of world looks and feels like.

In my ongoing battle with myself to trust my own knowing about such things, I received a daily reassurance from our three-year old resident Angel. She came into my room every morning for two weeks and picked up a book (no pictures) on Bible prophecies of the end times, thrust it into my hands and said, "read, read" and she sat next to me as I read it aloud to her for about one-half an hour at a time.

At this time, I am led to hope that there may be a shortening of this very difficult time. Events are starting to accumulate that suggest that Jesus may shorten the time and come back early. It is in the Biblical prophecies that this is possible and I certainly hope so. (See the Book of Revelations for more details.) Furthermore, it has been revealed to me that there is indeed one (among us all) who is designated as the one to hold the Christ vibration of All that Is. We first met on Mt. Shasta and two strangers came up to give us frankincense & myrrh. I still didn't get it for several months when it was revealed to me. He was in Jerusalem for a time serving Divine Will with his two brothers who are serving as "the two witnesses" of Revelations. There are many other Christed ones on Earth now, too.

There has been an acceleration of challenging circumstances for years, but this new millennium has been the most difficult that I have seen. Many people are in the throes of very difficult situations. Each is dealing with the most difficult and heart-rending, physical, emotional and psychological circumstances possible. Of course, September 11, 2001 changed things even more dramatically and the consequences are continuing in war, the economy, shock, fear and mistrust.

By 2002, it was not clear what worse could happen, but I have seen numbers of my good friends well one day and in the hospital fighting for their lives the next.

Following the devastation of Hurricane Katrina in New Orleans, Louisiana and the Gulf Coast in September of 2005, we begin to understand that these changes are continuing to escalate. We had the opportunity to see people in the direst circumstances and to see others respond either with compassion and assistance or with further outrages. We had the opportunity to look at ourselves and our values. We weighed ourselves in the light of this event. There was much room for improvement.

Mother Mary has come to me and a small group of devotees and requested that we pray daily. If you are moved to pray for yourself and others, please do so.

*Mary-Ma McChrist has recently completed the 7th edition of her prayer book, "**The Blessed Mother's Blue Rose of the Healing Heart**". I wholeheartedly recommend it to you. Go to her website at www.mother-matrix.com for more prayers and other details.*

Lord Sunanda has dictated this most recent analysis to assist us as we move through these troubling times. This was received in January, 2003.

Because Earth has moved onto two different trajectories since 1990, we would call your attention now to certain truisms and certain anomalies in the shifting and changing realities as experienced by you in form.

When Bill Clinton was elected President of the United States of America, a shift in paradigm occurred. Certain cataclysmic events did not happen. The dismantling of much that was fear-based could proceed. A global shift in consciousness could proceed. For eight years there was increasing prosperity, decreasing fear, increasing respect for the environment and many related events.

When George Bush took office in January, 2001, a second shift in trajectory occurred. The events of September 11, 2001 happened. Fear-based corrections were reinstated. Once again war was being promoted as an appropriate solution. Afghanistan was invaded. Iraq was invaded. The economy took a nose dive.

We would point out to you that the first shift in trajectory allowed us a glimpse into how things could be. The second shift in paradigm did not take us back to the same place because the preceding eight years had changed us.

We as a people are different now. We have memories of a different way. Now the choice is a real choice. We are clear that honoring the environment can really happen. We can make a difference in every area we choose to focus on.

Humanity is being faced with the same issues over again. Choose again for fear or for love. How will this period of tribulation emerge? What will the challenges we face look like? How can we best move forward?

Beloved ones, be at Peace, even during these uncertain times. The Peace you hold within yourself is what will bring Peaceful resolution to the world's problems. Fear and anxiety will not assist the world. Placing your attention on your highest and holiest thoughts will.

Guilt and self-flagellation do not raise consciousness. Blame and shame do not raise consciousness. There is no healing from dwelling on any form of negative focus. The only value to be derived from noticing negativity comes from focusing loving attention on it.

> *The Peace you hold within yourself*
> *is what will bring Peaceful resolution*
> *to the world's problems.*

During this time of "Tribulation"—or transition if you prefer—we are now releasing everything of the past as we step into a totally new paradigm and reality.

The coming Golden Age has been predicted for thousands of years. It will happen. How many will choose to align with the frequencies of Love is the only question.

We would point out to you that any delays you may have

been experiencing are because you are choosing to bring as many as possible with you into this new Golden Age. There have been many kinds of "assistance" so that there would be time and opportunity for healing to take place as extensively as possible.

When delays seem excessively frustrating, please pray for those whose lives, whose very souls, are being saved.

Update August, 2003: It has been announced by Lord Jesus, that the Earth has finally reclaimed the level of collective consciousness that she had lost, and is now again at the level that she held in the year 2000. We are also advised that the timing of all events is again accelerated.

Update January 8, 2005 - Beloved, I am Sai Baba.

We have held up re-publication of this book because there was material that needed to be added at exactly this time, so that the maximum number of people might receive these messages.

There are many things that will be happening in the coming years that may seem difficult or dismaying. We ask that you do not give in to the general attitude of fear or anxiety or worry that some new disaster might be just around the corner in your neighborhood or your country.

Rather we ask you to remember the simple Biblical injunction to give thanks in all things. We ask that when you pray for people give thanks that their God-Self, their guides and angels are arranging every aspect of their lives, or indeed their deaths, so that they might have the maximum benefit from the circumstances. That may mean karmic paybacks, release from old programs or beliefs or even that they might step through the last veils of illusion into the realms of Love and Truth and Light in the most perfect way possible for their individual needs.

Please also remember that what is true for others is also true for you. Your guides, angels and Higher Self are arranging everything for you so that the perfect circumstances are coming to you for your highest good.

Perhaps you have lost your job, have no money, are behind in your car payments and don't know how you are going to support your child in the coming weeks. There is no need to give in to fear in these circumstances. Remember that you have been cared for in the past and will continue to be in the future. You might laugh at the face of your current situation. It certainly isn't very pretty. Can you imagine that God will bring something good or even wonderful out of these circumstances?

Think of those who have lost their homes and perhaps even their families during the world disasters we have seen in the last few years. Was it through war or earthquakes, flooding or bombs? How can good come from this? We tell you that good is confronting evil every day. It comes from the neighbor who invites in a family who lost their home and arranges new clothing, food and furniture in a matter of days. It comes from the outpouring of love and money and food and service for disaster victims. These acts of love are touching lives and healing hearts every day. Perhaps only through such difficult circumstances can the deepest healing come to certain ones.

Please, every time something seems "terrible" or "hopeless" or "pitiful", remember that God is asking you to see this situation differently and to bring a new attitude and a new awareness to it. Please say a prayer of gratitude that God is working in each situation for the highest good of each one involved. Even as you remember to pray and give thanks your greater good is emerging, too, as you develop a whole new pattern of thinking and acting. Your prayers and gratitude join with those of millions of others and create a vast field of planetary love and blessings that millions and billions of others can draw on in moments of stress or direst need.

We ask that you pray and we ask that you bring your loving attention to those areas where you see a need. Do not help out of guilt or fear or shame or blame. Give the gift that you have to give to those who are in need. Can you give blankets? Do so. Can you give a million dollars? Do so. Can you give patient support and true listening? Do so.

More and more you will be placed in exactly the right place at exactly the right time to give the exact assistance that is needed by you and your particular gifts, talents or expertise. Begin to step out of old patterns of fear of rejection, fear of harm, or indeed any other fear. See yourself; truly see yourself. Call for the grace of God to heal that which holds you back and pray for strength and courage to boldly step forward into the perfect action that you are uniquely qualified to offer.

In so doing, you are building a whole new you. You are building a new human design for yourself. You are creating yourself according to the patterns of love and of beauty, of strength and of life.

As this "new" you emerges, you will eventually notice that you are happier than you have ever been. You will notice that at long last certain things that have bothered you your whole life have drifted away and shrunk to virtually nothing. You will notice that you feel so blessed to be able to offer that which truly feels real and right to others.

There is no need to look for the opportunities. They are being brought to you without any effort at all. The entire planet has stepped into a new paradigm and this time where there seem to be so many difficult situations confronting people every day is part of the transition phase. Bless this time and these opportunities. Bless and give thanks that each seeming difficulty is bringing more and more hope, more and more love, more and more healing to people on the deepest levels.

Bless those who seem to be creating difficulties for you. Bless them and give thanks for the circumstances that are confronting you. Each challenge is part of your stepping out of the patterns of the past and into a stronger, healthier, more loving, more joyful present.

Bless those whose beliefs and attitudes seem to be part of the problem rather than part of the solution. Bless their part in this great drama that is unfolding. Bless yourself for each situation that you face well, and for each one where you aren't very happy with yourself. Bless your growth, bless your challenges, bless your self in each and every choice and each and every moment.

Imagine, if you will, that you are surrounded by love. No matter the circumstances, no matter the perceived success or failure of the outcome. You are surrounded by a profound Love that holds the highest vision for your growth and awakening in this new world that is emerging. From time to time, remember to feel this love, to breathe it in, to be lifted up and to remind yourself that it is always there, even when you forget to notice.

This time of awakening is moving very fast indeed right now. You do not need to run to keep up. You do not need to surf the waves of change. You do not need to do anything complicated or difficult at all. Just give thanks and bless everything. This keeps you "going with the flow" in the easiest and most effortless manner possible.

We wish to say just a few more things before we close this section. We want to give thanks to you for the deep dedication and striving for the good you have brought to your life and to the Earth. We want to thank you for the years that you spent in the most difficult situations and the sacrifices that you made just to be here on Earth at this time. We honor you, we bless you, we give thanks for your lives, your service, your love, your Presence here on Earth.

Please continue to "hold the fort" during the coming days. We are gathering momentum at a rapid rate and soon you will see the changes all over the world that will tell you that, indeed, the Golden Age is truly emerging.

Now, take a moment, close your eyes after you have read these words and take a deep breath. Allow your awareness to move into your heart. Breath in the light that we are now pouring into your heart. Link your heart with the hearts of all Ascending humanity and allow the love to spread from heart to heart around the planet until all are filled and lifted up. Even in these most trying days as the ways of the past are being washed away, know that there is a spiral of consciousness that is being traveled by all; out of the old into the new.

All are now well on this path and the final remnants of the old Earth are being left behind. Perhaps through seeming disasters, but each seeming disaster is a reflection of another turn of the spiral and more people shifting higher and higher. The old patterns are being released, the new patterns are emerging. All is moving forward to the glorious new Earth.

Give thanks and bless yourself and all life. All is well.

Give thanks. All is well.

Chapter Two

A New Heaven and a New Earth

Lord Jesus/Sunanda Speaks:

We would speak here of what has been happening to you on Earth—of a larger perspective of Earth's role.

Earth's role in Cosmic evolution has been as a melting pot. All levels of evolution coexist here. We are here to teach one another and to learn from one another. We are here even to honor the consciousness and the soul essence within the whales and the dolphins; to honor the gifts brought by cats and dogs, horses and chickens, plants and rocks, earth, air, fire and water.

What Were the Soul's Lessons?

For some, the soul's lessons were part of their cultural heritage. For others, it was the work of a lifetime to gather one piece of understanding for the larger picture.

We are now at a time of change. The lower levels of consciousness will no longer be sustainable on Earth. Other planets will house those still choosing the lessons of density and duality. Only those who choose to expand in love will be able to remain.

What has been the purpose of all of this? Those here in Schoolhouse Earth have been learning lessons that will be of use throughout the solar system, throughout the galaxy—indeed, throughout the universe, and beyond.

You, who are in reality beings of vast levels of consciousness from throughout the universe and beyond, have extended yourselves as human beings on earth.

Those Beings which ensoul suns, galaxies and universes have taken form here on Earth to watch, to learn, to grow, to serve, to love. Those beings are yourselves. Each of your individual lessons, for better or worse, served the vast levels of universal mind in its evolutionary journey.

The sense of littleness, of separation, has been solely to allow a real sense of the experiences of your lives, rather than the sense of being a distant observer looking on from outside of things.

Each of you exists as a part of a vast continuum of consciousness through many dimensional realities. The circles around the body in Figure 2-1 represent levels of consciousness, and also the interface with the field of consciousness of great Divine Beings within whom we live and move and have our being. The individuality that you are is a Ray or individualized expression of God.

If you have expanded your consciousness, you might know your Christ Self as a Divine Being encompassing many individuals at that level. At greater expansions you might know your I AM Presence as a Divine Being also encompassing many individualities within Itself.

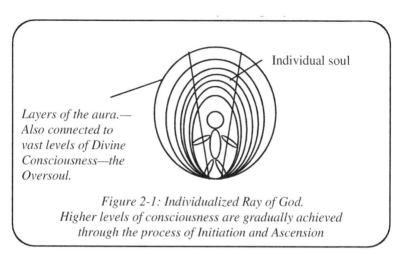

Layers of the aura.—
Also connected to
vast levels of Divine
Consciousness—the
Oversoul.

Individual soul

Figure 2-1: Individualized Ray of God.
Higher levels of consciousness are gradually achieved
through the process of Initiation and Ascension

The layers of the aura represent levels of consciousness or higher and higher vibrational states. As you take various Initiations, your conscious awareness moves beyond the restrictions perceived at the previous level. You become more expanded in your awareness. The levels are always there, but you are not consciously aware of what is happening at the higher levels until your have prepared yourself and taken various Initiations.

Furthermore, Great Divine Beings hold all that is within these levels of consciousness in their consciousness. Indeed, there is no difference between these Divine Beings and what we have been calling levels of consciousness. It is also to be understood that as you move into a given level of consciousness, you become more and more unified with that Divine Being. This is your spiritual lineage. That is, as you came into incarnation, you came through these dimensional levels and the consciousness of these Divine Beings.

Many other individualized beings exist within these larger fields of consciousness. For example, all the beings on planet Earth exist within the larger field of consciousness of the Being who ensouls the planet, the Planetary Logos; and that of the Being who ensouls the Solar System, the Solar Logos; and of the Being who ensouls the Galaxy, the Galactic Logos, etc...

As you Ascend in conscious union with the Higher Self, your point of reference shifts and you come to know, "I and the Father are One" (as first expressed by Jesus and recorded in John 10:30) and many now also experience: I and the Mother are One; I Am that I Am; I Am One with All Life.

Sai Baba, the Indian Avatar, describes it in a particularly clear way. At first we see ourselves as very small and separate from God, maybe so separate we can't even believe that He/She even exists.

Soul ◯ Separation   God

Eventually the longing of the soul for reunion draws us close. We still feel separate, and yet we know we love God and that we are loved in return. This is dualism.

Dualism   Soul ◯

Later, love and devotion lead to Ascension—union with the Divine. We know we are One—and yet God is still experienced as greater. This is called qualified non-dualism.

Qualified non-dualism

Through continued growth and expansion of our love and consciousness, we come to a full sense of union. There is no "other;" only One exists. This is unity.

Unity/Non-dualism or monism

We are never truly separate from God. But we can experience a sense of separation. We are now in the midst of the healing of the feelings of separation, loss, rejection, and abandonment that lie in our deepest soul memories.

What we are calling core emotional issues—the most deeply wounded parts of our psyche—are in our faces now.

There are those acting them out, and those repressing them. Ultimately, we must each deal with them.

The trial of O.J. Simpson that captured our attention several years ago was an expression of these core issues. It was part of a vast national and international examination of conscience. With whom did you identify? Truly, each of us carried all of the roles: victim, persecutor, rescuer, judge, jury, press, innocent bystanders, prosecution and defense, witnesses, record keepers, mass audience.

Why else would it have captured our minds? It was not just one man on trial. It was everyman, everywoman. It was not just one man's act, but the persecution of an entire race for centuries of actions, perceived or real. It was our deepest, darkest most wounded self screaming for recognition.

It is not about condoning murder. It is about recognizing that we each carry these deeply wounded parts of our psyche—our soul.

We must forgive ourselves and each other.

We must be willing to bring that part of ourselves out into the light; be willing to expose our pain and our deep wounds so that they might be fully and finally healed. We must equally find that place of compassion within ourselves to allow that bringing forth in one another. We must forgive ourselves and each other.

These deeply wounded parts of ourselves are not pretty and not nice. We haven't wanted to see ourselves like this nor wanted anyone else to see it. And yet, we must. To be healed, to be whole, as individuals and as nations, we must expose the wounds so that healing can proceed.

Bosnia is an example of the wounds exposed, and acting out on a national scale. Peacekeeping forces have allowed the release of energy without harm to others, much like a good therapist (unfortunately without the training).

There are answers, yes. Only one path provides healing here—Truth and Love. Not truth as we see it from a limited perspective, but Truth as God sees it.

The Truth of who we really are—the Truth that we are now and have always been deeply loved and One with All that Is.

Will we need to yell and scream and kick and punch as we express our rage, terror, fear and pain? Yes, and it can be done in a safe and a non-injurious way.

The abusive parent, friend, spouse or stranger needs to express these feelings without targeting any individual. Therapy is a must here. Few can find the resources in themselves, friends and family to heal otherwise. However, the therapist must understand these problems as Soul Wounds. It doesn't mean you are bad or awful. It means you are expressing what others are repressing; sometimes, because they are repressing. We all carry these wounds. Neither acting out nor repressing will lead to healing.

Healing will come when the Soul reestablishes itself firmly and finally in the Heart and Mind of God/Goddess/All that Is.

*Healing will come
when the Soul reestablishes itself
firmly and finally in the Heart and Mind
of God/Goddess/All that Is*

Those actions and behaviors which you are reacting to in others are denied parts of yourself. Healing comes when you acknowledge that you, too, are the murderer, the rapist, the abuser; when you forgive those parts of yourself that have such pain, such rage, such terror; when you allow yourself to love yourself; when you allow God and the Holy Angels to love you, comfort you, and free you from these patterns of distortion.

Those actions and behaviors
which you are reacting to in others
are denied parts of yourself

If this idea is foreign to you, I refer you to the writings of Buddhist monk and peace advocate, Thich Nhat Han, or to the songs of the New Age which remind us "there is only one of us here."

It is part of the distortion from the original phase of creation of this Universe and now embedded in all creatures of this universe to greater or lesser degree. Some might call it original sin; I am using the phrase "Original Cause." Do you think that this was error, or was it the intention of some vast being who watches the evolution of universes as our guides watch and assist us?

Whatever the cause, it is as though these parts of the Self have been caught in a sonic blast that left their etheric template seriously distorted *(See Figure 2-2)*.

For the most part, this is invisible both physically as well as in the normal course of events. However, if this distortion is triggered, you might see people both sending and receiving communication through the distortion. Have you ever wondered how someone could hear what you didn't mean?

From a place of distortion, it is virtually impossible to think correctly or to act correctly. The distortion affects your perception (what comes in) and how you act (what goes out). These soul fragments are part of your larger Self. There must be healing for the full Soul reunion and expression to take place.

Additionally, the distortion acts somewhat as a target for life events to reinforce the distortion.

This etheric template must be put back into its right configuration. To do this you can choose to be the Creators of your lives, constantly raising and perfecting each aspect that comes to your attention. Let yourself remember the original intention of this expression. All is to know yourself—what you are, who you are, who you are not. This has not turned out to be an overnight task. It takes willingness, time, attention and a lot of love. Set your intention that you receive all the assistance needed to clear this problem.

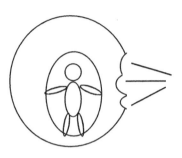

Figure 2-2: Soul Wound

Ask your Angels to bring to you the people, the places and the circumstances that will allow this restoration to wholeness with gentleness, ease and grace.

In *The Right Use of Will* series of books channeled by Ceanne de Rohan, you can find a further understanding of these issues. (However, please remember that human channels who bring through this information are rarely 100% accurate. You must use discernment in reading and exploring this material no matter how high the source.) However, Father-Mother God have committed themselves to helping us all through this phase. We must ask for the assistance to be given. And we must step forward and be willing to receive it.

(Author's note: On February 5, 2002, a group of Lightworkers gathered and corrected this distortion in the Universal template held by the Earth. We can anticipate more rapid clearing and healing now. This continues to mean to pray, to clear and transmute, to align with the Divine Blueprint of your perfection (located in the fifth dimension of your aura), also called your Holy Christ Self, and to look deeper and deeper at the real Truth of your soul.)

The Immaculate Conception

The Christian understanding of the Immaculate Conception refers to Jesus and his Mother Mary being conceived free from Original Sin. Another way of understanding this is a freedom from the soul wounds that carry this distortion from the time of the creation of this Universe. Jesus and Mother Mary were created without this distortion in their fields. They were then able to present to the world an Immaculate Concept of man and woman on Earth.

Mother Mary held the "Immaculate Concept," or the image of the perfect Divine Blueprint, for Jesus during his gestation and throughout His life. While he himself was born free, this enabled him to enter his ministry free from contamination by the soul wounds of others.

Jesus healed by aligning with the Divine Blueprint of perfection of each one he worked with—their Immaculate Concept. His ability to hold these patterns of perfection in his awareness enabled others to merely touch the hem of his garment and realign with Truth.

Father-Mother God are holding that image of our perfection for us. It is now Mother Mary's mission to the Earth to hold that Immaculate Concept for each of us in a very personal way. But we in form must take the responsibility for aligning with it. It is our free will that allows us to remain stuck in our distortions or to choose to return to the Truth of our wholeness.

There is a great deal more that could be said about these soul wounds. We leave it to those of you who are interested in this subject to expand further on the available information as it is key to the successful healing of the planet.

Resources:

All of the *Right Use of Will* series of books by CeAnne DeRohanne speak to this distortion in its various aspects, although that is not the only focus of these books.

Another excellent resource is the Diamond work of Fasil Muqaddam in Northern California. He refers to this distortion or soul wound as the "P." Books on the subject of the Diamond work are by Hamid Almaas.

The book *Don't Touch My Heart* tells the story of a little boy who exhibited the problems which we are discussing. However, it is not to be seen as an unusual and rare phenomenon, seen only infrequently. You must be willing to look within yourself to find your own "wounded child" and prepare a place where he or she feels safe enough to let you know that this wounded child is even there.

This is a work that demands all of your determination and willingness for others to see that you are not as perfect as you'd like. It takes tremendous courage to stand naked before friends and family or even total strangers. For far too long we have been unwilling to admit that the emperor has no clothes.

In so doing, you can then become that which you have been pretending to be. These wounds must be looked at clairvoyantly and may remain invisible until you are ready to deal with the issues involved. Someone capable of creating a safe space with you is invaluable when you need assistance.

On the other hand, when it is time for you to address these issues, it will be your great delight as well as your great challenge. There is no need to try to fix any part of yourself before it is time.

You will know when it is time, because it will be up in your face wherever you look. At that time, you will be ready to see what needs to be done and have the skills, tools and any needed assistance to clear it. It may not be instantaneous (or it may) but it will happen in a natural progression. Be kind to yourself, be gentle, be simple.

Chapter Three

Begin Each Day in Prayer

Beloved, I Am Sunanda
We will begin with prayer.

Morning Prayer

Oh Beloved Mother - Father God
I love you and I thank you
For bringing me every good and perfect thing.
Thank you for my growth, learning and healing.
Thank you for meeting my material needs.
Thank you for your Love and your Blessings
For myself, my family and all upon this Sacred Earth.
May I live this day aligned with your Perfect Will
As I fulfill myself in reflecting your Love,
Your Wisdom, Your Joy
In all I think and say and do.
For the Highest Good of all.
    Amen

I am your Beloved Child
One forever in your Heart.
       Mikaelah Cordeo

Prayer of Gratitude

Beloved Mother-Father God,
We thank you for the Infinite blessings
You rain upon your children.
We thank you for the birds, the clouds, the rivers,
    the ocean.
We thank you for the sun, the moon and stars,
And the light that shines on all.
We thank you for day and night, light and dark,
    large and small, the lessons of good and evil,
For all the yin and yang of our lives.
We thank you for the lessons of duality
And the Truth of Unity.
We thank you for Love, Wisdom and Power.
We thank you for Grace.
We ask that your mighty blessings continue
To Grace our lives with miracles,
Especially health, joy and prosperity for ourselves
    and all life.
We ask to always see your Love that gives
All things for the greater good.

Mikaelah Cordeo

*Add a short period of silent meditation on your Divine
Plan for the day—both what you expect to do and what the
universal mind will bring to you.*

Again a new day dawns, and you ask yourself, "What shall I do today? What is on my list of things to do? What are the surprises and the challenges that await me?"

We ask that each day, EACH DAY, you begin in prayer and thanksgiving to the Great Giver of All Life. Each day, look at the circumstances of your life and see the love, see the good that underlies all.

Begin Each Day in Prayer

Now, you might say, "My life is a mess. What do I have to be grateful for?"

We ask that you choose to see each day through the Eyes of Love. Look at the grander perspective, if only to know the great Love that enfolds you, even—especially—-when you feel your life is a "mess." Ask that the Love that ever holds you in a vision of perfection might help you to feel more of that beauty, grace, peace and perfection in your everyday experience. This practice also works for you who are already grateful to expand and amplify the good that already exists.

For you see, beloved ones, we are embarking on a great adventure here on Earth. As we amplify the frequencies of Harmony, Peace, Oneness and Love, we are anchoring Heaven on Earth.

We Are Anchoring Heaven on Earth

It used to be thought that Heaven was "out there" or "up there" somewhere, anywhere but where we were. Definitely someplace else.

Now, we are merging with Heaven. It is here, now. The only difference between those who know this and those who do not is a matter of attention and awareness. These thoughts coalesced into the following poem, published in *The Goddess Times,* Christmas, 1995.

A Christmas Poem
by Mikaelah Cordeo

And now the sun shines pale.
And light recedes too soon,
As we await the coming night
When Christ was born,
And with him, Love
To Light again our world.

No more the dark shall rule the world;
No more the Light shall fear to tread,
For separation has lost its sway
And God's Love wins the day.
As Christ is born in you and me.
We shall live forever free.

A new Heaven and a new Earth
Are being born, along with Christ the babe.
We watch in wonder at the pangs
That lead up to the birth.
Can such pain and grief
Really bring us all new life?

Does the mother remember such
When handed the little jewel
Wrapped in a pale blue cover?
Oh Lord, forgive our unbelief.

Slowly, slowly, I see Heaven descend.
Quietly, gently, I see Heaven blend.
Here and there, an Angel touches down
And spreads her glorious wings.
Here and there, I hear a song
And know what Heaven brings.

I know that there are wars.
I know that babes are dying.
And still I know that Christ is come
And soon will still the crying.

Begin to pay attention to the Radiance of Heaven in your life. The degree to which you see and acknowledge it, bless and give thanks for it, is the degree to which you are in Heaven.

That is, in fact, how you can define your level of consciousness. How much time is spent aware of God's blessings, aware of Love and Wisdom, aware of Beauty, Joy and Peace? The more constantly your consciousness is on the qualities of the Divine, the higher your consciousness is. Initiations into higher states of consciousness are a reflection of this. Indeed, an Initiation is virtually compelled by the need of your soul to be in alignment energetically with where you place your consciousness.

It is an ongoing process, this expansion of awareness. There is always room for growth, for there is no limit to Love.

There is no limit to LOVE

In these days of transition, it may seem that there is an awful lot of ugliness in our faces. Where is the Heaven in this, you may ask? The answer is that all that can no longer exist within the frequencies of Love is coming to our attention to be consciously healed and released—loved free.

If something you don't like is in your experience today, ask that Love and Wisdom fill you, that the energies of Grace and Forgiveness fill your heart and mind; that anything in you which drew this into your life might be healed, cleansed and purified completely. May every cell and atom of your Being, every particle of life be aligned with the highest and the holiest God design—your Divine Blueprint of Perfection—your illumined Christ Self.

In this way you will more and more anchor the frequencies of Heaven within yourself and release all that is less than Truth and less than Love. In this way does the Divine Alignment proceed.

What about free will, you may ask? Am I to become some kind of perfected automaton? Not at all.

This process of uniting with the Higher Self is one of greater and greater freedom—freedom to know, to grow, to love at ever more expanded levels.

You, as a soul, are free to choose limitation, pain and struggle, or expansion, joy and grace. It is like driving on a freeway. You are free to run into other cars or drive into the dividing walls and harm yourself and others. Generally, you do not choose to do this. Why? Common sense—or enlightened self interest. Usually, you choose, or attempt to choose, that which is of the greatest benefit to yourself.

This is just an expanded version of that—of choosing what is best for you in the long run. We cannot always see the bigger picture. So, align with that part of yourself, your God Self, which can see. This can help you to choose better, to choose the best. This is essentially a selfish act. But, because God Wisdom sees the whole, your Highest Choice is also that which is best for all concerned. This is what the Chinese have called the Tao, or the Way.

The Tao

There is a universal flow that is called the Tao. It is made up of the patterns and flows of energy of all beings. It is the consequence and the reflection of the choices made by all beings in creation. It is located in ninth dimensional reality at the heart of the three levels of the Divine Mother. (See pages 134 and 136 for more detail.)

The outer edges are chaotic, based on lesser, more selfish choices, while the smoothest flowing area is at the center, reflecting the higher choices which are aligned with the greatest good for all. This flow is such that when we are in alignment with it, we find things are all going our way. When we are out of alignment with it, we are "nudged" by life back toward the flow, like the monitoring system of a plane on automatic pilot.

But we are choosing to become conscious pilots in this

plane. So, the bumps and bruises of life are part of a system of checks and balances—the Law of Life—the Rules of the Game, so to speak, to maximize the opportunity for the greatest good for all.

Well, knowing the rules does make a difference. As Thomas Edison discovered, there are 10,000 ways not to make a light bulb. However, once he did find what worked, look at what has come from that hard-won piece of knowledge. Look at the thousands of uses that inventors have come up with to expand on that one idea.

Krishnamurti expressed it when he once said, "I am doing all this work so that you won't have to." You will build on these ideas like other inventors built on Thomas Edison's work. We do not all have to reinvent the light bulb. We can merely step into a room and flip a switch. The light is there as a help to whatever we are doing—working, sewing, reading, talking, inventing.

Each of you have performed hundreds of thousands of experiments to find out what works and what doesn't. Each of you has created a foundation of Wisdom, Truth and Love on which others will continue to grow and expand.

You are each a unique and remarkable combination of Grace and self-effort.

Look around at the millions of books on every conceivable subject. There is equal wisdom in each one of you. Each of you is capable of giving great service to life through the gifts you have to share and the skills you have acquired. You are each a unique and remarkable combination of Grace and self-effort.

We want you to know that this is how we see you. We see your beauty. We see your love. We see you and we love you.

Begin, dear ones, to see yourself. Look in the mirror and

say, "Oh my God! This is what God looks like. This is how God/Goddess has chosen to express on Earth. I can be—I AM—the hands, heart and body of God here to share my uniqueness."

Perhaps you will think, "Oh, dear, where do I start? How can I? I'm not nearly good enough yet. Maybe if I go to school two more years, four more, ten more, then I'll be ready. Maybe if I pray more, go to church more, join a monastery, I'll be good enough."

Imagine, beloved ones, that you are perfect exactly as you are. You are perfect for those you meet, perfect for those you live with, perfect just as you are. You have everything you need, right now, to do the tasks of the day.

You are perfect exactly as you are.

And there is still room for improvement. Mikaelah's favorite definition of Heaven is: In Heaven everything is perfect, and there is still room for improvement. Perhaps more school, or more prayer would serve you. Perhaps more play or more work would serve you. Still, today—this moment—is its own perfection.

Infinity is a very long time. Lots of time to explore all of the varieties of experience. What direction are you choosing? Right now on Earth it is time to go Home. The return journey into the Heart and Mind of God has begun.

It is time to go Home. Are you ready? The choice is simple. It is the choice to Love. Soon the frequencies of Love will be so strong that only those who love will be able to stay. This does not mean that those you perceive as dying did not love enough. But those who choose other than love, must find another planetary system in the denser frequencies on which to continue their lessons. Even they will take within their souls these last days on Earth when Love came to stay. They will remember. They will become the lovers in other denser systems. They will be the teachers—some future day. Their longing will be the call for the One Love to reach their systems of worlds.

So does Earth just blink out in a flash of glory? We won the galactic lotto game. What is next?

After the Ascension, What?

A famous Buddhist expression says:

> *"Before enlightenment,*
> *Chop wood; carry water.*
> *After enlightenment,*
> *Chop wood; carry water."*

The experience of living in a world does not go away —and yet things will be vastly different. You will be living and working side by side with those in a different reality for a while. Live so that others will wish to join you in the glory that is God-realization in the joy that is the expression of your own Divine Purpose.

The twinkling of an eye, when does that happen—or is this one of those 400,000 Earth years-one universal day things? The twinkling of an eye—for some, as individuals, you have already experienced this miracle. As a planet, that moment is still to come. There are quite a few surprises still in store.

You are perfect exactly as you are.

Chapter Four

Soul Star Awakening

Mother-Father God speaks:

We have come to you together today because it is well for you to know that there is Unity in the Godhead. The lessons of separation extended even unto the Godhead/Godheart of this Universe.

Duality was experienced here. This universe had taken on the lessons of Yin and Yang, positive and negative polarity, even good and evil, as was expressed on Earth by Adam and Eve.

We would speak to you, blessed ones, about this, for you are each an individualized expression—a Ray—of Our Essence. You have each explored these lessons through lifetime after lifetime, laying out the details of duality's curriculum, and now the time has come for graduation.

You have been part of a vast exercise in the exploration of separation.

You have been part of a vast exercise in the exploration of separation. As you migrated to Earth, the distance in conscious awareness between you and your Source continued to grow, until, finally, you explored life without full remembrance of Our Oneness.

Earth herself acted as a template for what was going on throughout the Universe. Every level of consciousness—

from the lowest (rocks and microbes) to the highest (Cosmic Avatars), from the most degraded to the most exalted were expressed here. Rama, Krishna, Buddha and Jesus are examples of the most exalted. Caligula, Hitler and Idi Amin are examples of its opposite.

You have each experienced separation from Source. Many of you experienced the sense of falling that took you into the various hell realms that outpictured here on Earth.

Beloved ones, your courage has been remarkable, but I say to you now, no matter how deeply you fell into forgetfulness, how far you distanced yourself in consciousness from the Godhead, still, I was. . . I AM with you always. Now is the time of the Great Return. We call you Home.

> *Now is the time of the Great Return.*
> *We call you Home.*

Earth has reached its apogee (its greatest distance) from Us. The return began October 11, 1977. This is a somewhat unremarkable date, but if one were to be given, this is it. For the first few years it was a point of stillness—no change could be detected. For your sense of time on Earth and ours in the Godhead are vastly different. One Cosmic day is many thousands of your Earth years. This has caused some confusion in the interpretation of your Bible.

Yes, we say to you, we do experience the passing of Time in the Godhead. We are also aware of the simultaneity of all things. But to learn of this and that, of cause and effect, requires a sense of beginning, middle and end, before and after. We, too, are part of still vaster consciousnesses that include other Universes. . . but that is yet another story.

Separation has taken many forms. If you have thought that God cannot forgive some terrible wrong you or another might have done, I say, "No!" I know that you are a part of Myself.

When a part of your body is injured, you do your best to save it. In extreme cases, you restitch whole hands or legs, with each vein, nerve, and muscle carefully reconnected, and you await the miracle I created in you of healing the separation.

Now, I call forth the miracle of healing the feeling of separation between us on every level of consciousness. On some levels of consciousness, there was never separation. It is from these levels of soul that you find your Guardian Angels and your Higher Self. Reach out for a moment to that part of yourself that never knew separation from its Source. That part of you, your Oversoul, holds the Divine Blueprint of your perfect image as you were created to be.

This is your Christ Self. In reaching out for that, you allow the Oversoul to touch you, much as Michelangelo painted God and Adam reaching out to touch one another. As this contact is made, you can allow a conscious receiving of the flow of Life. You can consciously allow the reconnection with your Divine Nature. See it as a matrix of Light all around your body, and ask that every cell and atom of your physical, emotional, mental and etheric bodies be fully connected into the Blueprint of your perfection. As you make this call, the cells and atoms of your body can begin to restructure themselves.

Exercise 4-1 Divine Blueprint: *(Say aloud:) "I now ask that every cell and atom of my physical, emotiona ʼ and etheric bodies (the four lower bodies) be fully c into the Divine Blueprint of my perfection. Thank* ɉ

Goddess. And so it is."

This can be repeated as you wish, not out of fear, but in order to reestablish true understanding at all levels of consciousness, even the subconscious with all of its conditioning. As well, repetition serves to expand this thought in the collective unconscious and becomes world service.

Now, we wish to point out to you that many have already consciously taken this step, and many others have done so unconsciously. Look around you at the numbers who have stopped smoking, switched from hard liquor to mineral water or carrot juice, taken up aerobics, low cholesterol diets, walking, jogging, organic foods. Self-healing and self-exploration have exploded onto center stage in the last few decades.

The trend will continue. However, to consciously choose not just a healthy lifestyle, but to reconnect every cell of your being with your link to Source will take you further than you ever dared to dream.

Jesus came to teach you what lies in all of you as potential. The ability to repair the body completely is in each of you now. The body is designed to maintain itself in health indefinitely. Up to now, you have been accustomed to seeing all around you die, often of horrible injuries or diseases.

*Some are now exploring the means
to fully Resurrect and Ascend
their physical form.*

Right now, there are those who are exploring what it means to fully activate their latent powers of healing and rejuvenation. They are exploring the principles of rejuvenation. This is part of the model Jesus presented and they believe it is possible to achieve exactly as He demonstrated.

The key principle is the power of thought, word and action. As you direct your attention to that which is a distortion of Divine Principles of Love and Truth, your body reflects that distortion. As you direct your attention to the highest and holiest (most whole) understanding of Truth and Love, your body reflects that.

As you direct your attention
to the highest and holiest understanding
of Truth and Love, your body reflects that.

One very powerful decree that can be used is: "I Am the Resurrection and the Life"...then add, "of my arm (my foot, my back, etc.)" This calls on the Resurrection principle in the Earth which is very strong in the Spring and at the times of the new moon. The Resurrection energy brings your physical body to its highest function at your present level of consciousness. It precedes the Ascension Ray, which raises you to your next level.

This is not an overnight process; for most of you it is a daily choosing. As part of our lessons in duality, we once had to choose between good and evil. Now the lessons are choosing between good and better and better and best. It is an incremental process.

Following the ideas presented through Guy Ballard's St. Germain Foundation and the teachings about the I Am Presence, some are now exploring what it would mean to fully Resurrect and Ascend their physical form. It is part of their journey of return to Source. There are thousands of you right now examining your lives, thoughts, words and actions and redirecting them daily, moment by moment, into greater and greater expressions of Love and Truth.

At a certain point in your journey, you merge with your Christ oversoul. There is no more separation. The journey continues as you become aware of level upon level of the Oversoul that is a vast continuum of Conscious Individuality back to Source and conscious Oneness with All Life.

Christ Consciousness is the link between the four lower

bodies (physical, emotional, mental and etheric) and the I Am Presence (holding Buddha Consciousness, Oneness with Father and Mother God, the Tao, the Holy Spirit). All are part of your Oversoul.

Jesus said: "No one can go to the Father except through Me." (John 14:6) This is what He meant. You must move from attention in the lower dimensional realms (physical, astral, mental etheric) into Christ Consciousness (5th dimensional) before you are able to pass into the realms of the I Am that I Am: the Father and the Mother (6th dimension and beyond). The I Am is a vast Ray of Beingness that extends from you here on Earth into the wondrous reaches of Divine Essence. You might think of it as your spiritual lineage.

That further state of complete Oneness with All that Is is what the Buddhists call no Self—no individuality. Yet you are here, now, in individual bodies with your unique gifts to express, your unique lives to live.

We wish to share a few ideas on these concepts of rejuvenation and God awareness. During the eons in which your Soul explored separation, certain patterns of involution were predominant.

Those energies and patterns which increased the separation and density of your experience were those you call negative: judgments, criticism, desire for revenge, greed, but, most of all, denial of your true feelings and acting out of distortion. These are often called vices, sins, or breaking the commandments.

That which brings you back to Source, back to wholeness, that which lifts you up, are experiences, thoughts and feelings of joy, forgiveness, peace, trust, hope, love, sharing, laughter; that is, the Virtues and keeping the commandments. We have been trying to help for a long time, you know, by giving you the simplest and the gentlest means for your healing and transformation.

Author's comment: In my own spiritual awakening, I found linkages with familiar and unfamiliar Beings: Jesus, Mother

Mary, St. Germain, Quan Yin, Lord Sananda and his oversoul, Lord Sunanda, Isis, and an androgynous being named Robert who is One in consciousness with Mother/Father God. This journey was not one of me looking into other religions. It was of my searching the depths of my Being to find God. What I found stretched me beyond the confines and expectations of my childhood religious training. I am sure that there is more to find, but Christianity stands me in good stead as I take to heart Jesus' injunction to love one another and learn to love that which had seemed foreign to me, and discover that it is my Self.

In speaking with others who found themselves on a similar journey, I found that we were part of those who had seemed to be mere myths—Zeus, Athena, Krishna, Quan Yin were parts of us in the vast reaches of Heaven. How could I despise another's religion when I am finding that it holds the answers to some part of my own Soul?

Soul Star Awakening

Scattered throughout the human population are some 10,000 Star Seeds, souls which represent the Central Suns of vast star systems throughout the Universe.

This is an interesting term—Star Seed. Just as a flower seed grows to become a flower, a Star Seed reaches a point of development and becomes a Star—a Living Sun. It is this phase of evolution that we are particularly interested in sharing with you. Though relatively few in number, your work will have its influence across vast starry distances. The time of shining expression has come.

Some of you know who you are already, others do not. Some of you have been preparing yourselves through various "light body" classes, workshops, Reiki, healing groups, self exploration, etc. Still others have been steadily working in less obvious but no less profound ways on self healing and soul expansion.

Those of you who have been drawn to the work of clearing and activating the "Ka" channels are in the phase which immediately precedes the Soul Star Awakening. *(Refer to the work of Amorah Quan Yin and Pleiadean Light work for more information on the Ka and the Ba.)*

For those of you who are not "Star Seeds," know that God's multiplicity of forms leave you an incredible array of possible expressions. Each of you are awesome in your own way for you as soul have chosen your own perfect path of expansion and expression within the Allness of God.

Messages of Light

Just as the last few years have seen the Earth receiving Light from throughout the Universe during its transition phase, so now the Light will begin to emanate from those Star Seeds whose bodies have accelerated, cleared, attuned and soon will burst forth as living Suns.

There will be 10,000 Suns of God shining from Earth. Collectively, they will link on inner planes and trigger the changes now coming to fruition within the Earth, and the Earth itself will begin pulsating Light-encoded messages back to Source.

Little or none of this will occur in the visible spectrum, but it will happen nonetheless.

What are these messages that will be broadcast? What is the meaning of this Light?

The Light, the messages, are part of the frequencies of health and wholeness that will begin to repair the electronic patterns throughout this Universe.

This Universe, in turn, will become a living Template filled with the vast motion of the starry patterns which in time will repattern the Multiverse.

The patterns of distortion, what you might call Cosmic Evil, have been experienced on Earth far beyond what anyone thought a civilization could withstand and still allow Love to prevail. Earth has been Crucified, Resurrected and Ascended. She has become a Cosmic Redeemer. These patterns of health will now restore a deeper level of health and perfection throughout the Multiverse. This is the work of the Melchizedek priests—the Star Seeds.

Many thought that Earth was the bastard planet—home for the unwanted and undesirable. Not so. Earth has been the hidden treasure. In your willingness to explore your darkness and bring Light to it, you have been the key in the transformation of this Universe, up to and including the Godhead.

There is a saying: that which hides in darkness will be your destruction; that which is restored to light will be your salvation. This is true now for Earth.

In 1999, the Melchizedek priests around the planet began to reset the Universal template. Some gathered consciously, others on inner levels. They will continue to monitor and to upgrade this grid as the final days of this era unfold.

How could there be distortion in God's creation? This is a good question. We do not yet have the full answer. It seems to have been an anomaly—an electronic wave that zigged when it should have zagged. Perhaps a pattern from ever more distant levels of creation than we are yet aware triggered within us all those patterns that revealed that which had a hidden flaw—and demanded its correction or it would ultimately lead to self destruction. Growth, ever-expanding perfection, is the Law of Creation.

> *Growth, ever-expanding perfection,*
> *is the Law of Creation.*

That which seems good and wonderful still has room for improvement. Becoming stuck in a pattern that is ultimately limiting will not serve the Divine Will. Thus systems and patterns exist, some as small as microbes, others as large as alternate universes, which will be drawn to break up those stuck patterns so renewal can continue.

Perhaps it is not yet time for our consciousness to have full understanding of all levels of creation. We can only grasp the level we have achieved and those which have preceded it. Earth is stepping forward into a new level. We don't really know what to expect. The vibrational frequency of this new level moves so fast we cannot perceive the details, much like the blades of a fan in motion seem to disappear.

Still, we know a little. It is the pieces of this vision of what is to come that we will be sharing.

Earth Changes

In the dim memories of our past—held in the etheric records of our planet, held in the myths of ancient peoples, accessed by intuitives—a story seems to have emerged.

Earth has gone through momentous changes. Land masses have risen and fallen, continents have broken apart, civilizations have risen, decayed and disappeared.

In Cosmic perspective the great periods of time are part of a larger rhythm. The ages of Pangaea, Lemuria and Atlantis have passed. The present age is in the midst of building to a point of great change yet again.

The predictions have abounded: Biblical prophecies, native people's prophecies, religious prophecies, psychic visions, etc. This time is recognized to be that which has been predicted: the End Times of the Bible; the end of this aeon.

Earthquakes, volcanic eruptions, weather changes are accelerating. What will happen? How bad will it be? Will we survive?

The exact details seem to be in constant change. Why? If you recall certain Biblical prophecies of destruction, you will remember that what would happen depended on whether the people heard and changed their ways or not.

People of Earth have been listening to the voice of their inner wisdom—God speaking in their hearts. This has been reinforced by news commentators, environmentalists, health educators and futurologists speaking of our need to clean up our act as individuals and as societies. People have been doing their homework, cleaning out their closets, healing the issues of past and present. In spite of what certain doomsayers have said about the way things are going, there is hope. Quite a bit of it.

The major wars and devastation that had been predicted are not going to happen. A nuclear holocaust has been averted. The superpowers are backing away from the brink of disaster. While there will still be changes and certain patterns are still being carried out, it could have been much, much worse.

For those who have been following the earthquake predictions, you will have noticed that there have been significant delays of what was expected, and what has happened has been much less severe than expected.

As 2003 opened before us, we saw contortions of expansion and contraction among the individual Lightworkers. The expansion occured as a natural function of the joy of extending your consciousnesses into new and delicious realms of Light, Love, Clarity, Wisdom and Bliss. The contractions come as new understandings confronted firmly held beliefs of the past, such as, "Oh, I couldn't do that! It's not polite, friendly, feminine, etc." or "I must follow my family rules to have a safe life." Or, "If I follow the rules (not my heart or inner wisdom) I will be o.k., safe, saved or loved."

Cataclysmic events such as earthquakes and hurricanes bring us face to face with our values and beliefs. We are able to look through the dramatic lens of such intense events at those things which we deeply admire and those which are clearly not working as we wish.

At first we must clearly identify that which no longer

serves us, that which is in contradiction to our deepest truth.
As well, at this point in time, old beliefs—religious, familial, social, etc. must be let go of entirely. Not because they are not of value, but because they were built during a time of limited consciousness. No matter how good, right or true they may seem, as you let go, you free yourself of the unseen limitations that were necessary as part of third dimensional consciousness and allow yourself to open to higher order understanding of the very belief you are releasing. Letting go of third dimensional constructs is vital for you to fully emerge into the fifth dimension. This step may require a good deal of trust and yet we encourage you to try this exercise—daily if possible. As the results prove their worth to you, you will know its value. The Apostle Paul once said, "by their fruits you will know them."

Exercise 4-2 Letting Go of Old Beliefs.

In the morning, ask your Higher Self to show or tell you which belief you are to let go of. Say aloud: "I now clear this belief of _____ from every record, memory, pattern and trace of my physical, emotional, mental, etheric and spiritual bodies. I call for the Angels of the Violet Flame to cleanse, clear and transmute this belief from my conscious, subconscious and superconscious mind. I let go. I let go. I let go. I cut all cords related to this belief and burn them in the Violet Flame back to their source. I free myself of all patterns of thought related to this belief and ask that all be thoroughly cleansed, transmuted and purified."

Now, gently scan your body. Notice if there are any areas of the body holding energy patterns that are related to this belief that would be served by clearing and releasing the energy.

Scanning: This is done in your imagination and is a very

powerful tool for self awareness and maintaining optimal health. Begin at your feet and gently trust your own knowing. Look for what appears out of place, dark, constricted, discolored or somehow "wrong". Slowly let your attention move from the ground up. Take one leg at at time if you wish or both together. You may notice a painful spot or a hot or cold spot. If you are more sound oriented, you may notice a change in tone or some discordance. You might see in the realm of colors or even get symbolic pictures. Trust yourself here.

Ask your Guides and Angels to clear any distortions and to raise to perfect health all energy patterns or configurations in your body. Cooperate with this by scooping, pushing out or pulling unwanted energy with your hands. Place it in the violet flame for the complete transmutation of all negativity as you remove it.

Call for white, gold and/or pink light to refill any areas that have been cleared or emptied. Consciously intend that you receive the highest order of new understanding related to this belief.

Say aloud: "It is so done. It is so done. It is so done. Give thanks: "Thank you God/Goddess."

We would like to give you certain understanding here. You, as individuals, have a physical body, an emotional body, a mental body, and a spiritual body or essence.

You are familiar with the physical body and with emotions and thoughts. But let us explain how they have an existence as real as, though slightly less tangible than, the flesh and bones with which you are most familiar.

Your physical body has a familiar structure. It also has an electronic pattern, called the *etheric double*, that fits right around your body and actually interpenetrates it. It can do this because it exists at a higher frequency than matter and can hold the same space without the particles bumping into each other. This is the *physical pattern* of the aura.

At a still higher frequency, the electronic pattern of the *emotional* (or astral) *body* surrounds and interpenetrates the physical. Those who can see these patterns report constantly changing colors as the emotions rise and fall.

Again, extending a little further out and also interpenetrating all the previous layers, is the *mental body* at a still higher frequency. These high frequency patterns of light around the physical body are called the aura.

The earth has the same kinds of patterns around her, composed of the collective fields of humans and other life forms around the planet.

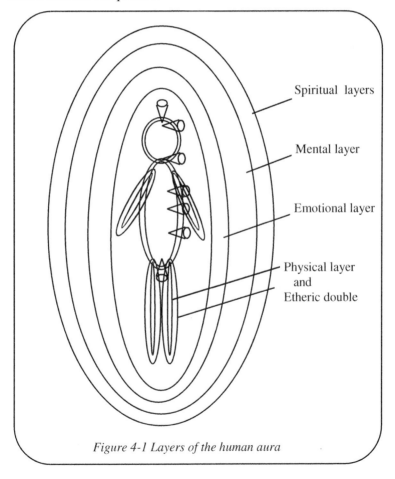

Spiritual layers

Mental layer

Emotional layer

Physical layer and Etheric double

Figure 4-1 Layers of the human aura

When there is distortion in your mental or emotional fields, it leads to an expression as disease or injury in your physical body and adds to the collective field around the Earth. When there is collective distortion on the Earth, it leads first to social upheaval such as breakdown of governments, undermining of social and moral values, and wars and eventually to major physical events such as earthquakes, famines, floods, fires and hurricanes.

When you work on yourself to heal patterns of disease and distortion at the mental level, it doesn't have to move into your emotional and physical bodies. When you deal with your emotional distortions and allow movement and healing, again it doesn't have to move into your physical body. If you become injured or ill and regain your health, this is another way to clear these distortions. If you and others don't work on healing your thoughts, feelings and bodies, then the Earth needs to do it.

When you work to heal patterns of distortion
at the mental level, disease or pain
doesn't have to move into
your emotional or physical bodies.

So, when you work on yourself and when enough of you do it, it actually changes the need for earthquakes, tidal waves, floods, etc., across the planet because it affects the planetary auric fields.

The vibrational rate of the Earth has been increasing rapidly since 1987. This means that those patterns of distortion, which we used to be able to tolerate when the Earth's etheric fields were denser, can no longer remain stable, and the patterns associated with them are disintegrating. That which was hidden is being revealed and many people are cleaning up their act.

Abuse is no longer invisible, ignored, acceptable or tolerated. Bigotry is out. The ozone layer has to be respected.

The oceans can no longer absorb our garbage. War is less and less a viable option of a sane people. We are learning the ways of peace, self-worth and more. Children and old people are being treated as worthy of care and respect. We are learning of our mutual interdependency with one another and with all other life forms.

There is still a long way to go. Some may feel as though they are running as fast as they can in this healing process. And still the pace accelerates.

You see, we must clear all patterns of negativity that we have ever expressed as individuals, as societies, and as a planet in order to step into this "New Age"—this Golden Age of Peace.

> *We are clearing all negativity*
> *that we have ever expressed in order*
> *to step into this Golden Age of Peace.*

The present geological patterns on Earth were created as a reflection of the massive distortions inherent in previous cultures. It is a natural and even a good thing that as we heal, as the Earth heals, the Earth will need to reposition and realign herself to reflect that health. And, no, we can't avoid Earth changes by staying messed up. These changes will happen, and all is for our ultimate good.

What we can do is to align to the best of our ability with the greatest health and wholeness we can within ourselves and in relationship to each other and all life. We can listen to our Divine inner guidance and follow the whispers and directions of God as we learn to listen with our hearts.

It is vitally important as the pace accelerates and the changes converge that we remember to pray and to bless life. There are many unseen influences that continue to suggest that we complain about or curse what is happening. If you aren't feeling wonderful, check for negative influences and clear, clear, clear.

Some have been exploring what it means to live in trust on God's promise to care for us always—as the sparrow or the lilies of the field.

Fundamentalists and New Agers have much in common here. They are equally dedicated to knowing and following Divine Will. The different methods can be right for those choosing them. Both can be right and valid. One doesn't have to be wrong for the other to be right, and both are probably making their share of mistakes as they are learning and growing from their choices.

The Planetary Christs

Thousands of years ago, 144,000 volunteers from Venus came to Earth to help hold the Light until those of Earth could learn to do it themselves. These are the planetary Christs, the anointed ones, found around the world. Looking at the planet as a whole, they can be seen as pillars of light, extending from Earth through the various layers of Earth's aura into the 5th layer. They each hold a focus of Light in the collective field of the Divine.

Now there are many more who have come to help and numerous others who have achieved this level of consciousness while on Earth. They all serve in the same way. Each of these pillars of Light are connected to the Christ Grid or Divine Blueprint for the Earth and serve as anchors or connectors to the Earth.

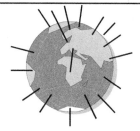

Figure 4-2: Points of focus of the Planetary Christs
Seen as pillars of light, extending
into the 5th layer of the Earth's aura.

This etheric pattern in the fifth layer of the Earth's aura is actually the Divine Blueprint which holds the new patterns for the coming era and completely replaces the previous pattern which had accumulated a good bit of distortion. This is much like DNA, which is supposed to self-replicate perfectly, but can become damaged by a variety of hazards as well as Time itself.

This new Blueprint is now fully activated and is creating a stabilization that is significantly different from the past. In the past, stability was a rigid structure. Those who sought to institute change were often the targets of persecution because it was known that the entire structure of society would crumble if too much change were to happen. This created enormous fear and resistance.

The new structure is growth oriented. As you open into deeper levels of unity, harmony and loving, you will choose to spend time in these new levels of expanded awareness.

Notice the delicacy and the beauty that is now calling to express itself. It is a time for extreme gentleness with yourself and others. For only in great safety and gentleness can this part of the self expand and open like the most delicate and perfect of flowers.

> *It is a time for extreme gentleness*
> *with yourself and others.*

At the same time, we will be experiencing outer circumstances that may seem to be the opposite of this safety and gentleness. We are being called to hold these qualities in our Beingness, so that the Earth herself might unfold and blossom. As we unite heart to heart and soul to soul around the planet, we strengthen one another in our ability to hold this new field.

Allow yourself to see the Network of Light linked through the hearts and minds of Christed ones around the planet.

Take time to rest in this new field of collective beauty,

gentleness, love and exquisite delicacy. It is not a place of fragileness, for those who have journeyed thus far are stronger than steel. The diamond brilliance of their beings have been purged in the fires and pressures of millions of years on Earth. We are daily refining and polishing the facets of our diamond natures. The rough edges are being polished, and every facet is being brought into the fullness of its beauty.

Holding this new frequency will create a stabilization around the planet. You may have been noticing that there has been a lot of change, seemingly chaotic at times. One day you are pulled this way, the next another, and the following, another way still. This seeming randomness of the flow is the result of the infusion of several rays or streams of light simultaneously, as well as the merging with dimensional frequencies not previously on the planet.

The new pattern will allow the new rays to blend and align with the matrix in a way that is harmonious rather than chaotic. The chaotic had the effect of breaking us out of stuck patterns; however, it also created a great deal of uncertainty. By working collectively to align with the new matrix, we together form the superstructure, the basic underlying pattern, upon which the more complex patterns will form (somewhat like weaving a basket or tapestry, or spinning a web).

These new patterns hold much higher frequencies of light than the previous structures were able to do. The effect is similar to that seen in the new papers that are iridescent or multicolored metallics. It is shimmering, moving, ecstatic, and yet there is a deep stability and purity of structure.

Thus, we will be able to have these qualities in our lives: more freedom, more movement, more ecstasy. New levels of aliveness and creativity will be able to be expressed without the need for society to repress them; because it will not create instability in the underlying structures, it will be in harmony with them.

In fact, the new structures will allow creative expressions that grow out of them and then beyond. As though a bird is first painted and then, given life, it lifts off the paper and flies into its own world, creating new patterns as it flies.

First, however, we must allow ourselves to hold the bonds of love between ourselves as we create the basic structure. We have all long awaited this moment—this building of the new template of our planet.

We must hold one another
with bonds of love
as we create the basic structure.

Author's comment: As I write this, I see we are just beginning to understand how we are all part of the Goddess, part of the Christ, part of the Father, part of the Buddha. What exactly is coalescing here on our planet? It is a mystery that is in the process of revealing itself to us.

Planetary Buddhas

Planetary Buddhas: The sixth layer of the Earth's aura is held by 15,000 Planetary Buddhas. Each one holds a collective field of focus that represents certain Divine qualities such as

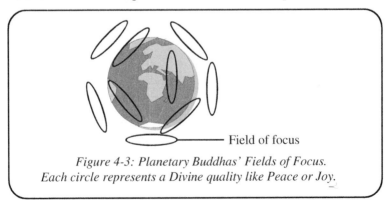

Field of focus

Figure 4-3: Planetary Buddhas' Fields of Focus.
Each circle represents a Divine quality like Peace or Joy.

peace, joy, gratitude and compassion. The Planetary Christs hold *points* of focus. Each Planetary Buddha holds a *field* of focus.

It is well to remember that we all have different terms for these states of consciousness. We must rise above the confusion that is created in our attempts to define/describe through language and attune to the sheer fabric and miracle of the Light itself.

Author's comment: Labor Day, 1997. I was writing about the second coming and Jesus coming on a cloud of glory earlier in the day. It had completely slipped my mind though. In the afternoon at the city park, someone pointed to the sky and said, "Look at that!" It was a cloud of a somewhat unusual formation for around here and even more unusually, it was radiating colors of pink and blue, gold and green in pale iridescent hues. Perhaps it was a phenomenon of the sun and I was seeing more to it than there was. But I felt that it was significant. My thought was: "signs and wonders." Later that afternoon I was up on Mt. Shasta at Panther Meadow, and this same cloud was still in the sky (the rainbow lights had disappeared after a few minutes earlier that day), but it was such a significant shape that I felt it must be something. I asked what it was and was told it was the command ship for Lord Sunanda.

Several years earlier, I had been reading about the Pleiadian ships that had been seen and photographed in Switzerland by Billy Meyer. I saw a cloud in exactly the same flying saucer configuration the next day. I felt it was a "hello" to me, but at the same time I knew that clouds are not space ships. So I wanted to know what it meant.

My inner understanding revealed to me that the ships existed in the higher frequencies, and the particles of water in the air were condensing around the electromagnetic fields of the ship, and thus the clouds were showing us the ships. Suddenly it all made sense. This is the same phenomenon that physicists use to study minute particles that are too tiny and too short-lived to measure any other way.

Physicists use something called a bubble chamber. They track the existence of these particles and their paths with bubbles which form around their trails. The bubbles last long enough for the scientists to measure. This was an explanation that made sense to me. I anticipate that some day we will all have a more definitive kind of proof.

I believe that it is in this kind of "cloud of glory" that we will see one aspect of the Second Coming. But I also believe that part of the Second Coming will take place within our hearts as we align with our own inner Christ presence, and that another part of the Second Coming will come as we collectively receive the Cosmic Christ in our hearts and learn what it means to be One soul, One body in Christ.

In May of 2002 I attended the Festival of the Christ celebration held in Denver, Colorado, which was presented by many awesome, God-filled beings. Following this event, the entire sky was filled with these rainbow irradiated clouds for many hours. This felt like a beautiful confirmation of this understanding.

I also believe that there is what I call a Cosmic Buddha Consciousness. This is also a collective experience. I was not raised Buddhist, and so I have too little of the traditional teachings behind me for them to be the foundation of my learning and understanding of what this might look like as it expresses here on Planet Earth. I believe that this may be an experience for another cycle of Time.

There is much that we do not understand about the great gifts that are within the traditions and teachings of the major world religions. It is a great privilege to be alive at this time and to see the unfolding and the blooming and coming to fruition of that which had been believed (but not understood) in the many religious traditions for centuries.

Chapter Five

Sacred Breath

Beloved Lord Jesus speaks:

Beloved Ones,
I ask that you know me also as Sunanda—Supreme Commander of the Earth experience—Avatar of Love.
I Am with each of you now as you read these words. Take a moment to feel my Presence. I Am a Living Expression of Love, filling and surrounding the Earth and all within and upon her. To know Me, to feel Me—merely ask to have the perfect experience for you now.
Many of you still carry extreme grief over experiences of your life. Some of this is experienced as pain or rage or shutting down of all feelings. Beloved ones, it is no longer possible to deny your feelings and remain upon the Earth. Experiences of pain are due to resistance to the flow of life. Ask now for the gentle clearing of these blockages and allow the Life, the Breath that is God, to move in you and through you.

Mini-exercise:

Imagine that each breath is searching the deepest recesses of your Being and freeing that which was blocked, releasing that which was bound, healing that which was wounded. Breathe now with me in harmony with the Holy Spirit—the Sacred Breath of Life. Breathe gently, effortlessly and deeply. Allow Life and Light to touch every cell and atom of your Being.
Gently close your eyes for a moment (after you read

the instructions) and just breathe—feeling my Love which awaits you as you continue to strive for right and to grow in the Light.

Many of you have made tremendous progress this lifetime. Others are only beginning your growth and expansion. For each of you, I personally guarantee that your lives will continue to grow in Love and Joy, Wisdom and Abundance.

I tell you now my Joy is expanding exponentially as I watch your growth and the manner in which each of you in your uniqueness share your precious gift of Life in your daily activities.

There is no—*absolutely no*—need to fear the coming changes on Earth. If I were to ask you to join me for an all-expense-paid trip to Hawaii, or your favorite travel destination, to meet wonderful new friends and experience marvels of serendipity and unexpected gifts you had long desired, I hope you would say, "Yes!" Your lives could not be better if you won the lottery, my beloved ones.

> *Only that which no longer serves you will be taken away.*

I tell you truly—from the depths of my Love—only that which no longer serves you will be taken away. What awaits you is greater joy, greater love, greater freedom, greater meaning, greater ability to live the life you previously could only dream.

Yes, there is a rite of passage, but even this time of seeming loss and change is a tremendous gift. Ask your own Divine Presence, your personal and direct link into the Allness of God, to grant you the willingness to release the past and to truly see the gifts that are showering down upon you each moment.

Focus not on what is wrong, but what is right. See the opportunities of your life for health, love, joyful growth, exploration, expansion.

Allow yourself to breathe in the Rainbow Lights of God Beauty, God Joy, God Creativity, God Faith, God Willingness, God Peace. The Earth is filled and surrounded with Light of such transcendent glory. Allow yourself the time to see it and to feel it.

Let the gentle caress of Angel wings fill your soul. Whether there is much or little healing needed, know I stand beside you. I Am with you every step of the way.

All that I say is Truth. Allow yourself to believe. You deserve it. You can have it. It is here now! Only doubts and fear stand between you and the experience of God's glory. Reach out and touch it. Take it in. Fill your cup at the endless Fountain of Bliss and drink.

> *Fill your cup at the*
> *endless Fountain of Bliss*
> *and drink.*

No drug, cigarette, or alcohol is needed to deaden the pain of Life. Turn instead to Me and release the painful memories. I will help you to clear the traces from your minds, bodies and feelings.

It is easily done; but you must ask.

It is your daily task, dear ones, this releasing of the past. In small increments it is done gently and easily. Make a commitment to yourself to heal, to bring forth your light. It is time. I call you now.

IT IS TIME. I CALL YOU NOW!

For those of you who call this Love I Am by another name, it will still work. Love is not limited to one form or one expression.

But, dear ones, make your commitment now to a regular,

daily practice of clearing for yourself and the Earth. For even if you have already achieved perfection, others can use your love and your prayers. And I tell you truly, there is no limit to the expansion of Love which is possible.

Each day is released to you a portion of Karma.

Each day is released to you a portion of Karma. Personal karma, family karma, national karma, racial karma, planetary karma. Or, in other words, each day you have the opportunity to transmute and forever cleanse from the etheric records any trace of misqualified energy that has ever happened.

This must happen now. It is happening now! Each one of you are doing your part, and the Earth herself is joining in this cleansing. We ask that you not judge these cleansings. Rather, join in prayer with the Earth and all life giving thanks that a new higher level of life is birthing itself upon the Earth.

I am asking Mikaelah to share with you two techniques for clearing. Both are simple but very powerful. The first method is working with the Violet Flame. You will find information and a helpful exercise in Chapter Eight. The second is working with Lord Jesus for your own healing and clearing. We will include it at the end of this chapter (Excercise 5-2).

The role of the Planetary Lightworker is to consciously clear planetary karma, cleansing the etheric records of the past, and reframing for himself or herself, and for the planetary records, the new thoughts and beliefs to be placed in the collective consciousness—the planetary mental body which is the third layer of the planetary auric field. This is composed of the combined mental fields of all life upon Earth.

The role of the Planetary Lightworker is
to consciously clear planetary karma.

The purity, integrity and perfection with which these thoughts are formulated and held determines the extent of influence that will be made at the collective level.

To the degree that these concepts are held to be of Value and Truth, they will magnify and grow, creating a field of strength and inspiration on which others can draw. These will be the foundation for greater understandings and deeper Truths to emerge.

Beloved Ones,

Be at Peace.

I Am Sunanda

ℰℐℭℛ

Mother-Father God–God/Goddess/All That Is continue:

Beloved ones, we wish you to know that we fully understand the concerns and fears that arise within you at the thought of Earth changes.

We are transmitting this information to you because it is vitally important at this time to have clear information. A few facts will make a world of difference in your ability to make this transition with maximum comfort and ease.

It is entirely possible that many of you will allow spirit to guide you to your own right place of protection and safety in plenty of time to avoid danger or lack of sufficient resources.

There is no need for panic as there are sufficient resources available for everyone to have a comfortable place to live and more than enough to eat, and all that is necessary even for an "opulent" daily life. By this, we do not refer to excessive waste or consumerism, but certainly all the resources you need to live joyfully with feelings of abundance and well being, will be available.

The first questions to ask yourself are: "Am I happy where I am?" "Do I find joy in my relationships with those around me at home and at work?" "Do I find myself longing for different work, more harmonious companions, even a different place to live?"

Listen to yourself. Are you feeling dissatisfaction with where you are, no matter how many times you try to make yourself wrong? Have you argued with yourself: "but it is such a great job or salary"; or "he (or she) is such a good person—we just don't seem to have any joy left in our relationship'; or "it's really very nice here, I just keep dreaming about something else"? Honor your true feelings within yourself. In fact, begin to honor your own truth and your own knowing of what is truly right for you.

Have you always dreamed of living in a mountain cabin or by a lake? Have you longed to drop everything and go teach or help in some way in third world countries? Does the idea of sailing the seas or homesteading call to you? Somewhere in these longings is the possibility of your future—a future with greater joy, more fulfillment and peace, more abundance in all areas of your life.

All it takes is willingness: Okay, God, I am willing to see where Spirit leads me. I am willing to let go of the safety and comfort with which I am familiar and to trust You to lead me to my own right place.

Now, I have to tell you. Some of you will be unhappy no matter where you go because you haven't entirely let go of the patterns of criticizing and complaining.

So, for your very first step in this process, start by honoring and being grateful for all the good things that are in your life right now.

For some of you, these old patterns were set down in childhood or in the face of the loss of some beloved person, pet or personal treasure. Perhaps it was an attempt to deal with fear of the future and fear of loss. "Well, if I just see how really bad these things are, it won't hurt so much to lose them."

Non-attachment is a wonderful achievement, but not at the loss of the enjoyment of each and every precious moment.

For it is only by being fully present and aware in this Now Moment that you can ever experience joy—or anything else for that matter. You can remember the past and dream of the future, but being fully present in your life right now is the only way to experience the treasures that are there for you.

Being fully present in your life
right now is the only way to experience
the treasures that are there for you.

Perhaps you will say to me: "but it is so ugly, boring and painful to do that." I say to you, only by staying aware in your present experience can you know what you truly desire and need, as well as, what is keeping you from having it.

Begin to listen to yourself. Maybe you have been so used to denying yourself, you don't truly know what you want anymore. Maybe you are so used to wanting what other people say you are supposed to want—and finding it empty and meaningless—you have lost hope of ever finding any joy in life. Maybe you have been so convinced that you don't really deserve anything good that you can't believe you could ever find it or keep it.

Whatever the reasons of the past that have kept you from finding and keeping Love, Peace, Joy and Abundance in your life, you can correct the faulty beliefs now. You can rewrite the script of your subconscious programming and create a life that is really meaningful to you.

I am not telling you that you will be able to change absolutely every bit of dross in your life into gold over-night. Even Rumplestiltskin took a little time spinning straw into gold.

For you to turn your life around takes time for introspection and time to adjust to new ways of living, thinking and doing things.

At no time in Earth's history has it been easier to do this. There are highly trained teachers and counselors and wonderful self-help books available everywhere. If you look around you will find supportive individuals and groups who are sharing this great time of clearing and healing the ways of the past. In truth, the greatest "Earth changes" that are now happening are those that are happening in the hearts and minds of humanity.

Take time for introspection and
time to adjust to new ways of living.

We don't wish to pass you off entirely to other hands here. We fully intend to offer you some worthwhile exercises and ideas for healing. We just want you to know you are not alone in this process.

Get to know your Guardian Angels

The first thing we wish to share with you is the idea of getting to know your own Guardian Angels. If your life has led you to believe that even your own Angel has abandoned you or given up on you, I tell you not only is it not true, it is not possible. If you are still alive, you are loved and there is still hope. (Of course, the same is true after you pass over.)

You are created of the substance and essence of God. You are made in God's image and likeness. You are a part of God, now and you always will be. Perhaps you have made mistakes or even made a total mess of your life. Nothing is beyond God's power of Love and Forgiveness. Perhaps you hate yourself and everything about your life. Use your hatred, rage or anger constructively. Ask God for help here to allow these feelings to energize the changes you want to make. Ask your Angels to bring you the help and the opportunities you need for healing and for change.

You see, the Angels must be asked in order to help you. And you have to allow yourself to believe that they will hear you and answer you. Now, I know not all of you will be able to hear or see your Angels right away. But they will help you anyway and they can bring you signs that they are working on the solutions to your situation, whatever it is.

The Angels must be asked to help.

Most of the help will come through normal everyday means . . . a phone call from a friend, an idea that leads to an opportunity, a book or movie or song that inspires or helps you grow.

If your life were to change miraculously overnight, you would still be you, and the beliefs and patterns which hold you back would still be there. It is these beliefs and patterns that must be looked at now and rebuilt according to the best you can dream right now. Once you learn the simple techniques, you can keep on upgrading. It's kind of like having a computer and upgrading it to a better system with more memory and better programs. It takes a little getting used to, but there is so much more you can do.

Really, your minds are very much like a supercomputer—and far superior to anything likely to be on the market in the foreseeable future.

ℰℭ

Exercise 5-1 *Meeting with and working with your Angels*

*Spend time every day getting to know your **Guardian Angel**. Sit quietly and start by focusing gently on your breath. Watch the breath as you inhale and as you exhale for a few minutes. Allow your shoulders and your back to relax. Allow your arms and your legs to relax. Allow your hands and your* *feet to relax. Allow a gentle smile to relax your face. Then think of one particularly lovely thing you might have noticed today or a favorite memory of something uplifting or beautiful. Ask your Angel to bring you a word or a picture, a sound or a color that is a link for you. Allow yourself to accept what you receive. Perhaps it is a quality of silence or peace, perhaps it is laughter or relaxation, notice and allow it to be what it is. Ask for a name to call your Angel. Trust this.*

Take the time to develop a two way communication link. Start off with simple things like what to buy for dinner. This builds trust and certainty for those times when you need help on more important issues. Enjoy!

Sometimes there is a need for particular help from the Angels. You may ask for Angels to bring Peace, Joy, Protection, Love, Comfort and all other Divine Qualities. See Chapters Six and Seven for more about the Angels.

Archangel Michael is very well known as a protector from negative influences. The following technique can be very useful if you are being bothered by negative thoughts or "dark clouds."

Calling Archangel Michael

Archangel Michael! (Repeat 3X) I call you and the Blue Flame Angels of Protection to surround and protect me. Completely remove and bind any beings that are less than the purest Christ Light from me and my home. Remove them from the Earth and all times, all parallel realities, all dimensional realities aligned with her at this time. Take them to their own right place to be healed and realigned with the Light of Truth and Love according to God's Holy Will.

I thank you. It is so done! (3X)

Please further remove and dissolve any negative thought forms and clear me, my loved ones, my home and my vehicles from any and all negativity.

I ask that I, myself, my loved ones, my home, property and vehicles be surrounded with a field of cosmic white light protection for the highest good for all concerned. I thank you. It is so done! (Repeat 3X)

Exercise 5-2 Healing personal issues with Jesus

Sit quietly and spend a few moments focusing on your breath. Imagine that the room is filled with golden light, with love, and breathe it in. Let all that seems painful or stressful be put aside for a moment and just focus on the breath as it comes and goes.

Then create a place in your imagination where you would be comfortable meeting Jesus. Perhaps you would feel best in nature with beautiful flowers or flowing water. Perhaps the image of a beautiful cathedral inspires you or perhaps you want to be in your own living room. Whatever you want is right.

Start by asking your own Higher Self to create a field of complete safety and protection around you and within which only that which is for your highest good may happen.

Then ask that your Guardian Angel be with you to help you to feel safe and comfortable. Continue to breathe. Ask that Jesus also join you as you work on a particular issue. For example, perhaps you had something very hurtful happen to you and you are ready to heal it. (If this is the first time you have worked with Jesus in this way, you may need to resolve some issue with Him or with Christianity. You may need to ask for another Divine Being, but it would be wise to clear any issues you have with Jesus as well.)

When you are ready to deal with your own issue, imagine that you are there experiencing it again, but this time Jesus is with you. Ask his intervention to bring the issue to its best conclusion.

Allow yourself to speak naturally and to say what you need to say. He certainly knows what you are thinking anyway.

By reframing your past experience with Jesus' Presence

and intervention, you will be creating new and healing memories that will help to clear the trauma from your consciousness. As well, Jesus will often create healing and cleansing miracles for those who call on Him.

(As a gentle warning, I wish to remind you that some people have difficulty with finding the real Jesus as their earlier programming was such that they believe that even He will punish or hurt them. If you do not find healing and love in this or any of the exercises, set them aside. You may need professional assistance to go further.)

Exercise 5-3 Gratitude and reframing

Sit in a comfortable chair and have paper and pen handy. Spend a moment just sitting quietly and listen to the sounds of the room and pay attention to your own body. Begin to notice the rise and fall of your breath.

Here is one of the ways you know God is always with you—your breath. God's life flows to you with your breath. Each breath brings life and vitality to your body. Each cell receives its quota.

Yes, yes, the air could be better, your body's ability to receive could improve, but right now, just as you are, you are receiving, you are being nourished, you are being filled with Life with every breath.

So, we start here. Gently say, "Thank you." Thank you for the miracle of my body. Thank you for the Love that comes to me in so many ways: the freedom to live my life, the freedom to make my own successes and failures, the freedom to change, the freedom to be whatever I can dream.

Notice any part of yourself that wants to argue. "But the air is polluted; my body isn't perfect; I'm not as free as I want to be."

See what is going on for you right now. Do you spend more time arguing than being grateful? It is all right. We are not judging you. But it is important to pay attention here. The degree to which you are grateful, versus resisting or arguing, is the degree to which you are now allowing God's gifts, which are all around you, to be received.

Think about it. A child living in abject poverty can still find joy in a mud puddle or watching a puppy. Peace does not have a price tag. Love is the very foundation of all life. It holds the atoms and molecules of life together as well as filling and surrounding all that lives. Can you see it? Feel it? Appreciate it? That is the question.

So, ask yourself, "How much am I willing to receive right now?" Imagine a cup. How full is it? This is what you are allowing yourself to have right now.

And now pick up the pencil and paper. Write down the first five reasons that come to you of why you can't have the things you want (for instance):

Not enough money.

Everybody's against me.

Nothing I do ever works out.

Life is too complicated. I can't figure it out.

I don't know where to start.

Now, imagine a magic genie or fairy godmother within you, touching each thought with a magic wand and changing it to its opposite.

I always have plenty of money.

Everybody helps and supports me.

Everything I do works out.

Life is simple; I figure it out better every day.

I start each day with gratitude for the Love,
    Wisdom, Power, Authority and Clarity
    that flow through me.

And so on.

You will be able to use this simple exercise many times in many ways, and it is wonderfully useful to share with others also.

Please don't argue,"but it's not true!" Your idea of truth is relative to your perspective. My Truth may look quite different from your "truth." If you want to know what is really True, start imagining how God sees things. He/She/We see the basic goodness that is in all things. We see your basic goodness striving to emerge through all the circumstances of your life. We see ourselves in you and our special patterns of gifts and abilities that only you have. We see your courage, your love, your strengths. And in all the parts of yourself you call your failings, we see the hidden strengths there as well.

We see your tremendous striving to move forward, no matter what the circumstances of your lives. Even those you perceive as evil are trying to do the best for themselves, however distorted or limited their vision.

So, we have taken a step together, and I want you to understand that this is a giant step. To consciously read these words and follow these instructions is a giant step.

"It is?" you might ask. "What do you mean?" Well, how many times have you thought, "God, why don't you make it easy? Just tell me what you want. What am I supposed to do? Why can't I hear you?"

Have you ever felt like screaming, you were so frustrated? Well, we have certainly heard you. We are honoring your wishes here. Those who can hear us are sharing our words with you as clearly and as honestly as they can all over the world. That which used to be reserved for the very few, the "chosen" ones, is now accessible to all who desire it.

Classes abound in learning to speak with Angels, Guides, Higher Self, God. If you don't want to do it yourself, there are books, tapes, and public presentations where those who serve in this way pass on heaven's messages to you.

You are still required to be discerning for the vehicles are still human. They are not always 100% on. And you have your own filters of how you hear and interpret things. So, even the best information must be carefully and honestly dealt with. If it doesn't jibe with your belief system, don't force yourself. On the other hand, you don't have to reject everything that you don't understand either. You can set things aside. Perhaps time and experience will give you a way to understand later, even if the understanding is only why something is unacceptable to you in a larger context.

But back to why this is such a big step. It is because you are choosing to find out what is really true for yourself. And you are choosing to trust God (through these words and in many other ways) to bring you the help you need for growth, healing and all the needs of your life.

Exercise 5-4 The Creative Breath

Again sit quietly. Notice your breath and remember: at the other side of every breath is God. It is kind of like playing ball as a child. God throws you the ball. You catch it and throw it back.

You breathe in God's gift of life. Take it in, fill your cells, release back to God. In breath; out breath—filled with and surrounded by God.

Now, choose just one aspect of your life where you want to see more Freedom or Joy or Love or Abundance or . . . (fill in the space with some other God quality). Breathing in God's Love and Joy and Freedom, direct it into that part of your life. Breathe it in, release it; breathe it in, release it. You are creating a partnership with God here. You have an idea of what you want and God has an idea of what will best fill your desire. Together, fill your heart and mind with the Light and Love that will bring to you all the people, things and circumstances to bring it about in the best possible way for you and anyone else who might be concerned.

Does it seem too simple? It can be this simple. We could make it more complicated for you. But this is all that is necessary.

Breathe in; breathe out— asking that your desires for a better life and God's vision for you come together to create even more than you ever dreamed. And remember to say thank you in the beginning, in the middle and at the completion.

We thank you for your love, your strength, your courage, your willingness to take on the challenges of life, and to take these steps into greater unity and harmony with God and all life.

We wish to close by offering this simple advice from an old Amish saying: You need to pray **and** move your feet.

You Need to Pray
AND
Move Your Feet.

The perfect life isn't just handed to you on a silver platter or watched on a TV monitor. It is an interactive experience. You need to respond to the opportunities that come to you. You might make some choices you like less than others. It is OK. Life is a process. The end is just that, an end as well as the opening to a new beginning and more choices, more opportunities

With Great Love we now close this section.

Chapter Six

Guardian Angels

Mother-Father God speaks:

Beloved Ones, there is quite a bit of misunderstanding about what is and what is not a Guardian Angel. Your Guardian Angel is a part of your soul essence—a part that is clear. It is established in the higher realms of consciousness and can, therefore, be of assistance to you who are in the denser realms where there is so much confusion and distortion.

Some people feel that those who have loved them and

then died have become their Guardian Angels. Your true Guardian Angel has been with you since your conception. It is a life-long assignment of deep love and commitment. While there is one primary Angel assigned at conception, others may be added depending on your mission.

Those who have died may also be serving to watch over you. Husbands, wives, parents, aunts and grandparents, may have an Angelic nature, and may indeed be watching over you. But the position is more as a guide or assistant.

Your true Guardian Angel is always with you. This is their only joy for the duration of your life.

Their growth, their learning is linked to the assistance and the love that they give to you. Your Guardian Angels are watching over you always, whispering words of encouragement, suggesting the best ways for you to accomplish your day-to-day activities as part of your larger mission.

The primary thing that you should know about your Angels is that they want the highest good for you. This does not necessarily mean how you can have the nicest car, the most money, or the richest or most handsome lover, but what is best for your growth as a soul.

What you as a human being see as a "good" thing, isn't always what is perceived as "good" by your Higher Self and your Guardian Angel.

To give you an idea of their work, imagine if you will, that you are a Guardian Angel. Let us imagine that your human charge is a three-year old child. You are a direct conduit of God's love—indeed of all of God's gifts for this child. It is up to you to work with other Angels who are overseeing the larger picture. It is your job to be aware of the goals to be achieved in a given day—lessons to be learned, karma required to be experienced, people to meet and interact with, as well as the larger life mission toward which all must build.

Constantly in your mind is the question: "Does this serve

the larger goal of the soul and the soul's mission?"

Your task is to give support, reassurance, advice and love to assist the overall attainment.

And you must be there, present and aware, loving and ever ready to assist, no matter how serious the trouble, how difficult the life, how little the human self appears to want your guidance and your help.

Even as young as three, the child is frequently the target for darker forces, seeking to thwart the soul's growth and mission.

You can guide, guard, protect and inspire, but you must not interfere with the soul's free will. For it is the lessons gained from the consequences of choices either in harmony with or in opposition to Divine Will—the larger Plan and flow of Life—by which the many facets of the individual soul are purified and refined.

The desire for unity with the Diamond Matrix of the Soul is forged in the fires of Life.

Only in complete oneness with the Soul's Blueprint or Divine Pattern of Perfection can there be the complete flow of joy, love, wisdom, etc. Here is the soul's goal—-reuniting ever more perfectly with its own Perfection—the Holy Christ Self, the I AM Presence, the Buddha Nature.

Each lifetime has been a further refinement of the lessons needed for soul growth.

The very young child is often aware of the Guardian Angel's Presence and its Love. As the child grows older, the sensations of the physical body and the world more and more claim his or her attention.

The very young child is frequently attuned to the elemental kingdom also. Children often see and talk with the fairies. They are also very often able to speak with their Angels and to speak of deep soul truths. Some remember moments from their time in heavenly realms or past lives very vividly. This is particularly true of those children who have been born in the last ten to twenty years, and is often a matter of some surprise to their parents.

At about the age of seven, often called the age of reason, another level of consciousness is fused with the child's awareness. New levels of karma are able to be dealt with, new lessons are able to be absorbed. Going to school is part of the recognition and reflection of these new levels of learning now presented from the larger world.

Again at twelve to thirteen years of age, another level of consciousness, the next level of complexity, is integrated. At this point begins the final stage of preparation for dealing with karma and the completion of the soul's purpose (unless the soul is choosing an abbreviated life span for some reason).

The hormonal system kicks in, and the final integration of the emotional body and the mental body is made.

The adult personality is set as a complex mixture of the infant, the three-year-old, the seven-year-old, and the twelve-year-old. The memories, beliefs, and experiences of training, culture, experience and family tradition become part of the whole complex with which the individual soul must work.

Through all the experiences of the years, the Guardian Angel works ceaselessly to maintain a linkage of loving advice and support.

In the busy life of a teenager or a young parent, this linkage can be mighty slim indeed. Where are the moments of quiet attunement necessary to listen? They are few indeed when one is focused on the external reality.

Precious and rare are the ones who strive constantly to maintain this link with Heaven through all the circumstances of their Earthly lives.

Not all label it God or Heaven or Angels. Some call it Peace or Conscience or Human Values. Whatever the terms that describe this human link into the realms of the ideal—it is life's goal to forge these links.

It is your Guardian Angel's work to assist in every way possible in the awareness of the sanctity of all of your life.

No matter what your circumstances, you have the opportunity to extract the good, to focus on Love and to expand your connection with the Divine.

Take a moment now to look at your own life from the larger perspective of your Guardian Angel. See the loving arms that held you steady as you learned to walk. See the wings that sheltered you from the worst of life's storms, while still allowing you your experiences.

Can you say thank you to this faithful companion? Can you realize that this seemingly separate being is really a part of you—of the larger Self?

If you as Soul know yourself as an individualized aspect of God through many dimensional levels, you may experience your Guardian Angel as separate from you—a unique expression of Divine Essence, but they are indeed part of you, the Soul.

In this merging with the Divine that is now happening on Earth, you are being given the opportunity to unify with greater and greater aspects of your soul—your Higher Self or Oversoul.

Your oversoul might be individualized into many lives or individual souls at this time. Indeed, some of these individual souls may be in several bodies. It is from the level of the Oversoul that decisions are made as to which soul qualities you will have in a given lifetime (your strengths and weaknesses, your personality) and which soul lessons you will deal with—which elements of karma you will face.

At this point of planetary and cosmic evolution, many are merging with the Soul and the Oversoul into higher and higher levels of Consciousness until reaching the fields of Unity.

At the levels of Cosmic Christ and Cosmic Buddha, of God/Goddess/All That Is, your individualize I Am Presence knows its oneness with all other Individualized Presences. You may find yourself knowing a level of oneness with certain people that you know here who are also consciously attuned at this

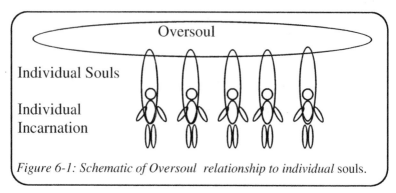

Figure 6-1: Schematic of Oversoul relationship to individual souls.

level. As your consciousness expands and your level of awareness increases, this attunement with those of similar vibrational frequency becomes more evident to you in your daily life.

As you advance, higher and higher levels of the Self, of
the All, serve as the guides, teachers and Guardian Angels,
until eventually you know and experience All as One.

And even in these vast realms of Unity, there are levels
of growth and expansion available.

And there are many different kinds of Angels—different ways of expressing Divine Essence at various levels of
Consciousness.

Many of you are awakening to find your attunement with
the Angels to be such that you are realizing that you are of
Angelic consciousness in a human body. This certainly creates a few surprises for you. And yet you know it is true. Yes,
there are beings from every level of consciousness on Earth.
It is part of the vast experiment that is underway here.

Angels

What are some of the different kinds of Angels (one author calls them angles) of God?

Angels—The general term is also applied to a specific
category of Angels. These are the Angels that carry the specific Divine Qualities under the supervision and direction of
the Archangels. Each is responsible for distributing a certain

degree of a particular quality such as Love or Hope or Faith or Trust or Mercy. Perhaps it is a tiny angel, somewhat new to the business of bringing grace to the world, who shares a smattering of Hope or a dash of Faith. Perhaps it is an Angel with more experience, and therefore more authority and more capacity, who brings you a deep wave of Peace or reassurance or fills your heart with Love. Each are called by your prayers and each shares according to his or her capacity.

Archangels—Beingness capable of expressing on every level of consciousness, hence God's messengers who serve in bringing forward the Divine message wherever it must go. In this universe, the Archangels also serve as representatives, or holders, of the different Divine Rays or qualities of God. They are also divided into male and female aspects as part of the overall experience of duality in this universe. The Archangelic consciousness extends far beyond this universe as well, but that will not be discussed here. They are also linked with the El-ohim as creator Gods of this Universe. This can be discerned by the names of some of the more well known Archangels: Micha-el, Rapha-el, Uri-el, Jophi-el, Gabri-el. (See page 93 for the names of the Archangels and their feminine counterparts for the Twelve Solar Rays.)

Thrones—serving in the exalted levels of overseeing vast systems of worlds, these are also known for their constant attendance at the throne of God. They are always God aware.

Principalities—galactic overseers also serving on Earth as part of the vast array of Angels in charge of the larger scheme of things; e.g., watching over the flow of civilization's patterns, overseeing the role of religion in society. We would like to indicate that it is through the infusion of certain key "seed" thoughts through the ages that mankind has grown and developed. These are the beings who oversee the appropriate timing for the appearance of major and minor Avatars and also prepare the way for the large outpicturing of vast Cosmic dramas on the stage of our human lives on Earth.

Elohim—the builders of Universes. The Creator Gods/ Angels. In this universe, these beings are also in male-female polarities and associated with particular rays: Peace and Aloha, Purity and Astrea, Arcturus and Lady Diana, Hercules and A-Rubea to name a few. There is quite a lot of esoteric literature that refers to them if you wish to study this further.

The Elohim are also a part of us and they have been merging with their human bodies which have prepared themselves by conscious attunements, meditation and prayer, during the decade of the 90's. They are embarked on a vast Cosmic initiation of their own at this time. In simple terms, we would describe it as the successful coming together with one another in conscious unity and the co-creation of that which is revealed to them through their unified state.

This task is complicated by the fact that they are also outpicturing the "wounded child" core issues which we have referred to before. They have taken on certain vast human patterns (planetary thought forms) for healing. So, you see addictions, sociopathic tendencies, and various kinds of human disease patterns, such as cancer, multiple sclerosis and mental illnesses from schizophrenia to bulimia and suicidal tendencies, all alternating with their Divine aspects. Each individual is only dealing with one of these patterns, but none of them is easy.

This makes working together a decidedly difficult proposition at times. Learning to support and trust one another without being co-dependent, victim, persecutor or rescuer is challenging to say the least. The work of the Elohim reached a key point in 1999 when they began participating in the co-created re-setting of the new Universal templates. This continues on into the new century as they began co-creating the embodiment of the Councils of Light on Earth.

In the preceding one hundred years we demolished many of the old patterns of marriage, family, education and society. Now we must come together and choose what we wish to keep from the past and add our new ideas, visions and dreams for the future. The New Templates of Society for the Golden Age must be built by conscious choice. What are our values for home, family, culture, education, business, religion, government, economics, music, art, health? Every facet of society has been examined. Now we must choose the highest and the best we can envision and point ourselves in the direction of our choosing.

Aeolah—These vast Angelic consciousnesses exist outside of this universe. They have described themselves as those who incarnate as Elohim to create universes. Thus, their cycles of Being are vast beyond our ready comprehension. They, too, have blended with their physical counterparts on Earth. Again, the names are an indicator of this soul essence. You might see a lot of vowels which are indicative of various frequency specializations and spiritual lineages. As well, the "ah" ending is common. This is seen in many Biblical names such as Rebecca, Deborah, Micah, Judah, Isaiah. These ones in human forms are often well aware of themselves as Divine Expressions. Having the name is not the only indicator, but it is a definite link into the spiritual lineage.

Seraphim—A classification of certain advanced Angelic training. They serve primarily as teachers and are part of the Solar Angels, though this ranking can be achieved in a variety of Angelic categories. On Earth they are often visionaries and mystics, as well as being scholarly and philosophical. They are said to have a fiery quality to them. Some of the famous saints of the Catholic Church were of this category, such as St. Dominic, St. Catherine of Sienna, and St. Augustine. Their work is education on a vast scale.

Cherubim—This is another subset of certain vast Solar consciousnesses. These groups of Angels serve as templates, if that is not too strange a word in this context. That is, they outpicture certain divine patterns within their being. Such patterns or concepts as motherhood, brotherhood, goodwill to man are more complex than a singular quality like peace or joy, which are deeply complex in themselves.

These beings are also serving to work on the vast re-patterning of the planetary thought forms. They are frequently engaged in planetary healing work on the inner planes. In their human lives you might see them in such persons as Albert Schweitzer, Fritz Perls, Fritjof Capra, and Mother Frances Cabrini. They are often engaged in large scale humanitarian efforts.

Golden Solar Angels—Brought to our attention by Solara in her books, these great Divine beings are from the Godhead—the realms of God/Goddess/All That Is, in the Great Central Sun. Here we see Divinity expressing on Earth in the form of Jesus, Buddha, Krishna, Isis, Quan Yin, St. Germain. Now, we feel it is important to clarify that these beings are really beyond our ability to describe in the scope of their Consciousness and their Beingness. If you have ever had the privilege of conscious connection with any of these, they have revealed only a portion of their vast glory to you.

And, yes, we each have the opportunity to align with this Oversoul aspect of our Beingness. Thus, if you know yourself to be an expression of Jesus, Maitreya, Quan Yin—then you are blended with your oversoul which is operating from the Godhead.

Again, there are vast, innumerable levels of consciousness within which you might have made these alignments. It is best to take all such wonders of God's Plan for our conscious reunion with our Divine Essence with great humility. A little humor doesn't hurt either.

We all are of these lineages. Some are consciously aware and attuned, and others are not. And there are vast levels of attunement that can be achieved. That is the only difference.

We would like to point out to you here that there are vast realms beyond All that Is. (I, Mikaelah, have not explored them and will be able to give only the briefest of descriptions of two. The idea of vast realms may seem a little strange at first thought. All That Is sounds pretty inclusive. But our

language has limitations in its ability to describe these vast Cosmic states of Being—No Being.)
   Light of Infinite Being—the Being Li-A-Ron came to me from this level. This androgynous being described it to me not so much as a place as a Way. From this level of Being, the desire is to walk the paths/patterns/the Way of creation/void, and to ensure that distortion is identified and corrected. This is in alignment with the work of the Melchizedek Angels/priests.

Melchizedek himself (androgynous) is a Consciousness of such vastness that it is hard to describe what we are dealing with. Joshua Stone identifies him as the Logos of this Universe. This would mean that he is holding the vastness of the Universe, all levels of consciousness and all beings within it within his own consciousness. And that He is considerably more than that, as that would be equivalent to one of your lifetimes on a vast cosmic scheme.

Ground of Infinite Being—I (Mikaelah) was recently taken to yet a deeper level of experience in what are perhaps the Buddha realms. (I say this because a gifted friend and artist drew the Being who came to me from this level as an Emerald Buddha.) At this level you will find the templates and grids of creation. Here you will find the Flower of Life Pattern as presented by Drunvalo Melchizedek.

The Flower of Life Pattern in its various parts and configurations is the foundation of creation into form. It holds the templates for all that is made manifest.

So there is a lot more happening on Earth and this Universe than any of us are likely to be able to wrap our consciousness around. And beyond that is vastness beyond my words to describe. For those few who would have an interest and a need to know more, you will probably also have the ability and the tools to allow your own personal exploration.

Now, for those who say that Jesus is the Name above all other names, the Lord of Lords: I cannot argue with you, because I have not come to a place where His vastness stops and some other Being's goes on. I have experienced the vastness and the Love of Mother-Father God, of Quan Yin, of the Buddha, too. I also know that these Beings are not in a competitive mode. They operate in such vast states of Unity, that we would be fooling ourselves if we thought we had more than the tiniest grasp of Who they are and what they represent. In following the teachings of these Great Ones, we will never go wrong. In trying to prove that one is bigger or better than another, we are way off the track of the Love and the Wisdom that they taught.

If you think that because God exists as a Trinity, that that is all there is to God, you are putting limits to something that is Infinite in its expression. At this time it might be inspirational to look at the Trinity of the Masculine expression and the Trinity of the Feminine. See the two triangles coming together. In the merging of the two, you will find the lovely and highly potent symbol of the Star of David. Take the triangle of the lower chakras and the triangle of the upper chakras and merge them in your heart in a Star of David and just be with the experience for a moment.

That which was long worshipped as the Goddess is not in opposition to the Christ or the Buddha. All aspects of the Divine are vast and also interwoven in ways both glorious and mysterious. To exclude the Goddess and the Buddha from Christianity is to cripple it. To exclude the Buddha and the Christ from the worship of the Goddess will do the same. We are all called to expand our consciousness to include far more than we ever dreamed. There is no limit to Love. God says, "All are beloved." There is no part of creation more loved than another. There are those parts only able to open so far to love, but even that is subject to growth. A seedling receives proportional to its need. A full grown plant needs more and receives more. An eighty-year old tree again receives according to its need.

Chapter Seven

The Angels and the Rays

Archangel Michael speaks:

The Angels are those aspects of the soul which remain unblemished in the Heart and Mind of God/Goddess/All that Is. They did not bring their consciousness into the denser realms. Rather they are of assistance to us on our return journeys.

They each are expressive of certain rays or Divine qualities. God, of course, in His/Her multiplicity expresses an infinite variety of qualities/tones/rays. We will be dealing here with the seven original (or planetary) and five (formerly secret) new qualities or rays (now part of the twelve rays coming from the solar system). Each of these also have many gradations, as blue or red exist in many variations.

First let us introduce the Archangels of the Rays. We will also be dealing with the new solar ray colors. These have an iridescent quality to them. Please note that there is so very little information on these rays at this time that those who are writing about them may have connected with different Angels and/or experienced different colors.

We also point out to you here that these rays or soul qualities exist in a variety of colors, not just blue or yellow or pink. However, as they enter various frequency bands, certain colors predominate.

The original spectrum on earth was represented by the seven colors of the rainbow and the seven notes in musical scale:

do-re-mi-fa-so-la-ti-(do). These were part of just one solar ray.

As the Earth's vibratory rate has increased, the frequency band we are now working with is that of the Solar system and includes 12 major rays—each of which includes the range of the original seven. That is, each has a complete rainbow within it. Thus, you may find differences in people's interpretations of which Ray is which color and varied experiences with the Rays and what they represent.

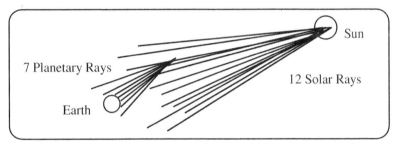

Figure 7-1 12 Solar Rays and 7 Planetary Rays

It is the nature of the Archangelic presence to be able to journey successfully across many frequency bands. Alice Bailey describes the current work of the Ascended Masters as they are now returning to form to demonstrate dominion on all rays and all dimensional realities. In completing this, they will successfully merge with their Archangelic self and complete the full twelve rounds of the Angelic or Solar evolution. They will then move on to greater service as Melchizedek Lords.

During this phase, there is also the re-uniting of Twin Flame Essences prior to full reunion with the God (Logos) of this Universe.

We would point out to you that, simultaneously with these individual events, there is the coming together in conscious unity of the soul bands as part of certain Oversoul frequencies.

Thus, there is the re-uniting within the 12 soul bands, represented by the 12 apostles and the 12 tribes of Israel.

Figure 7-2: The Angels and the Solar Rays

Ray	Color	Archangels	Divine Quality
1	Blue	Michael & Faith	Will
2	Pink	Chamuel & Charity	Love
3	Yellow	Jophiel & Christine	Wisdom
4	White	Gabriel & Hope	Purity/Ascension
5	Green	Rafael & Lady Regina	Healing/Science
6	Ruby/Gold	Uriel & Donna Grace	Devotion/Resurrection
7	Violet	Zadkiel & Holy Amethyst	Freedom/Forgiveness
8	Aqua	Aquariel & Clarity	Certainty/Clarity
9	Magenta	Anthriel & Harmony	Synthesis of 1-7
10	Gold	Valoel & Peace	Peace/Opulence
11	Peach	Perpetiel & Joy	Joy/Serenity
12	Opal	Omniel & Opalescence	Transfiguration

(Archangel names curtesy of "Take Chare of Your Life"
Vol 9:9-10, P. 13, Aug. 1993)
*Lady Regina, an Archangelic aspect of Mother Mary, took this
role, when Mother Mary moved to a larger Universal role.

Ultimately, there is also the reuniting with the Christ at the 13th level which is also the Melchizedek level of consciousness. We will not go into this further at this time.

The Buddhic pattern of reunion proceeds a little differently, working through the various traditions and the concept of Sangha or fellowship. Ultimately, these two great streams will merge both on the individual level of uniting with the Christ and the Buddha in the heart, then the balanced relationship with an equal partner, and ultimately the reuniting of the entire Christ-Buddhic family—the Love-Wisdom Band.

We would like to note here that the Buddha and his 999 followers who attained enlightenment were a complete soul group and their collective Ascension marked a key moment in Earth's history.

The Buddha (Lord Gautama) is the Oversoul Consciousness for all 999. The 999 are the Oversoul Consciousnesses for tens of thousands of others. Certain Tibetan thankas, or religious paintings, show the Buddha and the hundreds of smaller buddhas beneath (within) him, which is a representation of this concept.

Tibetan Tulkus, or reincarnate lamas, are these Buddhas returning lifetime after lifetime to aid and assist all living beings in attaining their own enlightenment. There are unrecognized others, of course, located around the world who also serve in this way. Not all are formal Buddhists, but rather they serve in all traditions.

This is what it means to be a Boddhisatva, one who has completed the cycles of birth and rebirth on his own behalf, but returns to help until all sentient beings are free.

Within the Christian tradition these ones are often recognized as saints. If you read certain Christian literature with an esoteric perspective, then you begin to recognize certain elements which are called one thing in one tradition and another in a different one.

Christ as the Open Door

The concept of Christ as "the Open Door" is an Initiatory concept. When you open your heart to the Love that is the Christ, then it is as though a doorway appears through which you can step into the next frequency or dimension. You may continue to remain here on Earth as well, because all frequencies are now interpenetrating one another on Earth.

We would also like to point out that there is also a change in the proportions of the different frequencies on the planet now. The denser frequencies are decreasing proportionately as the new, higher frequencies are expanding. For example, if before the denser frequency A was 80% and the higher frequency B was 20%, now A might be 50%, B, 30% and a new, still higher frequency, C, 20%, where it was previously too small to measure. Thus, just as many are taking individual Initiations in consciousness, the Earth is also expanding its collective consciousness, and all benefit automatically.

The strengthening and anchoring of the higher frequency bands onto the Earth has been part of the activity of various Lightworkers and planetary healers.

As the light and frequency levels continue to increase, it also serves as a Cosmic Wake Up Call. As the Earth reaches a certain frequency, waves of souls begin to awaken and re-align in full conscious awareness with the Truth of their own nature. Even very exalted souls, though, are for the most part untrained in working with these subtle energies. (We will be adding information to the website: www.mcordeo.4t.com for a list of the kinds of teachers, trainings, books and exercises that are invaluable for the newly awakened.)

All information can be accessed on the inner levels. You already have all you need to deal with whatever issues you face.

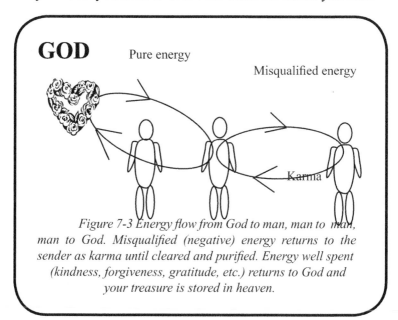

GOD   Pure energy

Misqualified energy

Karma

Figure 7-3 Energy flow from God to man, man to man, man to God. Misqualified (negative) energy returns to the sender as karma until cleared and purified. Energy well spent (kindness, forgiveness, gratitude, etc.) returns to God and your treasure is stored in heaven.

Understanding certain principles of action and familiarity with the full nature of what you are dealing with will, however, simplify and ease the process of the final stages of transformation and transmutation In order to complete this process that is now in full swing, we must requalify (restore to its original purity) every iota of energy that we have ever misqualified on this planet in any lifetime .The principle is that God sends us pure energy that we are to use and qualify with our own unique set of gifts and talents. The energy then returns to God in a cycle of Love. When energy is misqualified (e.g., with distortions of rage, hatred, lying, etc.) It cannot return to God. So it continues to be sent out and then to return to us until we get the lesson, heal the problem, transmute and purify the energy, clear the karma. When the energy is cleared, it can then complete its return journey to God.

> *We must requalify every iota of energy*
> *that we have ever misqualified*
> *on this planet in any lifetime.*

Many are also working on karmic issues at a galactic and universal level. This is our task now in order for this planet to complete its Ascension process. We must requalify all for which we are responsible. This responsibility is not limited to personal karma either. It can also include family karma, racial karma, national karma, planetary and even galactic and universal karma.

Examples of family karma include child abuse repeating through generations, certain forms of cancer, hearing or vision impairments, poverty, etc. Examples of national karma might be the effects of slavery, racism, or colonialism. Examples of planetary karma might include denial of and attack on the Divine Feminine (also universal karma), destruction of the environment, atomic bombing (polluting Earth and outer space).

Examples of Universal karma might include errors resulting during original creation, the Luciferian rebellion, experiences of Separation from God resulting from duality, experiences of God as violent or punitive, denial of the emotional body.

Many are working on karmic issues at a galactic and universal level. Beings from throughout this universe exist here on Earth in physical form. On inner levels you are directly linked to various stars, planets and galaxies in this universe. And each of those stars, planets, galaxies, etc. are ensouled by Divine Beings. You might think of that as your spiritual lineage. Earth is a microcosm of the changes happening throughout creation. The work done here affects the entire spiritual lineage that you represent. There are also many representatives of the Devic Kingdom, such as elves, gnomes, fairies, etc. in human form at this time. They have their own lineages and all are working on aligning with the greater whole. All are part of the great plan of God now being made manifest on Earth.

General Principles
When Calling for Divine Assistance

Use the Violet Flame: The use of the Violet Flame of transmutation and forgiveness is one of the key elements in this transmutation process. *See Chapter Eight.*

Ask for Assistance: Another key element is to ask for and obtain heavenly assistance. In order to obtain heavenly assistance, the first rule is You must ask for it. It is the Law that there can be no usurping of free will, and that Law is followed by those of the Light.

When calling on the Angels and various Divine expressions, such as Jesus or Mary, Krishna or Buddha, it is recommended that you say the name three times.

This creates a vibrational frequency band or link from them to you. The first call gets their attention (so to speak). At the second call, a wave of attention finds the location of the caller. The third call enables the clear linkup. Often, when we are in constant communion with an Angelic helper or Divine Being, one call is sufficient, but three is considered a safety factor. Another protection is to ask if they stand in the White Light of the Christ or the Violet Flame of St. Germain. You may then ask or command that which you desire.

Divine Will: Certain general principles apply. Ask that all that you request serve the Highest Good for all or be in alignment with Divine Will, the Divine Plan or Purpose, and that which serves the whole best will be achieved. Focusing only on what you personally see as ideal may call forth more limited good and ultimately may have unforeseen (and unwanted) repercussions.

Highest Good: Asking on behalf of another must be according to their Soul's highest good and choice. For example, healing of the body before certain lessons have been gained or despite the soul's wish to leave, does not always serve the highest good of the soul. It is usually the human personality that feels an attachment to having things work out a certain way. The Highest Good is that which is best for all concerned.

Another area where there is often some confusion is when our idea of what seems best for a friend or child is not the best for them in the long run.

Prayers for others may be specific or general, but always according to God's will for the individual and their individual soul's choices as well.

Blessing: If you perceive that another is unable or unwilling to receive what you desire to give, you may ask that it be held for them etherically as a blessing when they can receive it or have need for it.

Thus, prayers for safety, protection, love, healing, etc. can be held until needed or appropriate.

Chapter Eight

The Violet Flame

Lord Sunanda begins:

We will be speaking briefly of the Seventh Ray of God-Freedom and Transmutation, the Violet Flame. In the past, there were five (of the primary seven) ray energies which would be considered of major influence during different time periods on Earth. These five always included the first three (Will, Love and Wisdom) and then, two of the remaining four rays would vary, with one phasing in as another phased out over vast periods of time. This was part of the Cosmic Cycle or Cosmic Clock. The seventh ray— the Violet Flame or Violet Ray—is now phasing in, and the sixth ray of Devotion is phasing out. That is, the energies of the Sixth Ray are decreasing in influence and those of the Seventh Ray are increasing. This is increasing the qualities of freedom, forgiveness and transmutation of negativity available to be used on the planet.

It was to prepare the world for these energies that Jesus taught his disciples the principles of forgiveness. And now it is for the purpose of healing and transmutation of all negativity that the information on the use of the Seventh Ray energy, the Violet Flame of Freedom and Transmutation was released by the Ascended Masters. Gradually the information has been shared with thousands—millions around the planet. It continues to be necessary to work with this energy to heal and transmute the past as we prepare for the future. This is the same energy that Jesus taught us to use when he preached of forgiveness. The power of Forgiveness is Violet Flame energy. St. Germain is the Ascended Master who first introduced the information about the Violet Flame to the Earth. He has long been known as the Chohan of the Violet Flame. That is, he holds the office of the highest teacher of this energy on the planet. Quan Yin, Goddess of Mercy, held the office before him. St. Germain, and many of the Ascended Masters, have moved into new duties, but St. Germain is still very much associated with the Violet Flame. The Archangels that are associated with this Ray are Zadkiel and his Divine Complement, Holy Amethyst.

(Author's comment: This next section is one of several written several years prior to the main body of this book. Mother/Father God specifically requested that all such sections be inserted. This one is based on my years of working with St. Germain and the Violet Transmuting Flame.)

Exercise 8 -1 Working with the Violet Flame

I like to encourage people to work with the Violet Flame as often as possible because it is so very powerful and comforting. Fortunately, it is also quite a simple matter. A daily clearing of yourself and your home is not too often. I have found that regular clearing of house pets is also valuable as so many of them work as healers for the family and sometimes take on energies that they cannot easily clear. This will lead to better health and longer lives for your pets.

Ask for Assistance: *One simple and highly effective way to work with the Violet Flame energy is to sit quietly and ask for the assistance of the Angels of the Violet Flame. Lightworkers often call upon St. Germain as well. It is Divine Law that these beings must be asked by ones in form in order to assist. St. Germain does remind us that **he is not the Violet Flame**. We are to learn to invoke it and to work with it ourselves. However, there is no harm in calling for assistance in the learning stages.*

__Give Thanks__: Spend a moment giving thanks for the Love and the Blessing of these Beings of Light in your life. Knowing these Beings and working with them so directly is one of the great gifts of God to Planet Earth.

__Violet Flame:__ I frequently recommend imagining a small campfire of Violet Flame at your feet. Send every disharmonious pattern, energy, thought or feeling. Even physical pains or problems that you wish to have completely cleared and transmuted may be sent into the Flame.

For example, if you have a pain in your arm or another part of your body, imagine sending this pain and any memories associated with it into the Flame to be completely transmuted into perfection. If it is connected with some interaction with another person, you may be holding their thoughts or feelings in your arm. Send all energy which is not yours into the Flame to be completely transmuted into its original pattern of perfection.

You might know that the problem you are working on has been in your family for generations. It might be a genetic problem or a behavioral problem such as child abuse. This is family karma. You may ask for help in releasing all patterns of this problem from everyone in your whole family lineage, past and future—as well as present. Send all of this into the Flame.

__Planetary Healing:__ You may realize that this is a problem affecting your entire nation or throughout the world. You may similarly pray for assistance in passing this whole pattern of imbalance that resides in the physical, emotional and/or mental bodies of the Earth through the Violet Flame. If you feel drawn to do this larger work, it is very valuable. Frequently, people struggle with clearing the same issue over and over again. It is because they continue to draw on the planetary thought forms of which their problem is a part. Those have been created by all humanity over thousands and thousands of years.

The Violet Flame transmutation exercise can release tons of discordant energies from the Earth, freeing all life from its disturbing influences.

Refill with Light: *When energy has been released from your body or your energy field, it is important to replace it with new, positive energy, or the empty space may attract other negativity to refill itself. (Nature abhors a vacuum.) You might wish to fill yourself with the Light of a Golden Sun, or imagine your Christ self / Buddha self / I Am self pouring forth a rainbow of Light and blessing into you. You might wish to speak out loud a statement of health and wholeness, reflecting your highest vision for yourself with respect to this issue and your life.*

Why: *Those who know how to do something of value are needed now. All who are willing are being called to assist in this way. Those who answer are doing a great service. Every part helps. All who serve are blessed most mightily.*

∞CR

Author's comment: *I have been asked if this is not too simple. I can only tell you that I have used this method for many years, and I am still amazed at its power and effectiveness. One can clear any type of misqualified energy in the seven lower dimensions with it. Many things that might have bothered you for years can be completely cleared. If you find that it isn't quite intense enough call for galactic or universal Violet Flame which is more intense still.*

Occasionally, I am required to use gold light in order to work on higher order problems, but very rarely. For those who are most accustomed to working with white light (which includes all colors) that, of course, is always appropriate.

If you find that you have difficulty imagining the colors that you prefer, know that your intention is what is most important. You have called for violet, and it will be so, whether you see it or not. With more experience you may find that it was always there; you were just not paying attention to it.

A call to prayer. *As we entered the period referred to in the Bible as the Tribulation, I began to hear from lightworkers around the world that there were some important concerns. Without creating undue alarm, I would like to point out that there are some significant differences in what needs to be done for our individual and collective safety now. I believe that the way in which people across the planet responded to the events of 9-11-01 was an indication that we have learned the lessons and we do turn to prayer, to service, to acts of love and compassion for the most part.*

However, what I want to point out most urgently is that we are now responsible for making daily calls for the protection of ourselves, our loved ones, our homes, our work, our country and our world.

We are asked to take on greater awareness and responsibility for the safety and protection of ourselves, our loved ones, our projects and so on. Angels no longer automatically watch over airplanes and cars. They must be asked. Where once we were the unconscious recipient of a great deal of Divine care and often intervention, that is no longer an automatic given.

Obviously, there is much that is still watched over. We are not yet ready for consciously controlling major factors in the world such as rotation, gravity, and so on.

Do not take this responsibility lightly, nor be afraid to take this responsibility at all. Make a commitment to pray for all that you hold dear. Pray for Lightworkers around the world who are working tremendously hard to deal with their own deepest issues and that of the world. Negative influences often lead them into moments of hopelessness or feelings of being unloved, unworthy or useless. Your prayers make a difference. Make a commitment to pray and decree for a healthy and loving world for yourself and all life. Be specific or be general, but do pray regularly.

Furthermore, events have demonstrated that there is

much change and turmoil coming to us now. We can expect it to increase in intensity. Since the harmonic convergence, that has been the pattern, increasing intensity. Take the time to center and to create a loving and gentle space for yourself and the deep healing and clearing we are all doing.

Chapter Nine

The Cosmic Clock

Lord Sunanda speaks:

At this time there are several Cosmic time periods coinciding. You might think of it as several different clocks which all have different numbers of hours striking 12 at the same time. Now you can imagine that a clock with 12 hours and one with 100 and one with 10,000 and one with 100,000 hours would not strike the same time too often. That is what is happening now on Earth. All of these Cosmic Clocks are striking the same hour. The timepieces of the Universe, however, are not made with dials or digital readouts. The timing devices of the Universe are the cycles of the stars and the planets.

Thus, Earth has time related to its daily rotation facing the sun and turning away from it (24 hours) and its rotation around the sun (one year). The solar system also rotates on its own orbit and we have a 26,000 year cycle with every two thousand-plus years a different set of starry constellations coming into prominence. Thus, we have the Piscean Age, the Aquarian Age, etc. This is also known as the *Precession of the Equinoxes.*

Each of these star systems reflects its own unique combination of Light, which is its gift from the Creator. Their personal contribution by virtue of the sum of many individualized aspects of God within each system and their "qualification" of energy is their return gift to the Creator. Thus, the uniqueness with which each is qualified, its particular rays and gifts, has more or less of an effect, depending on its relationship to other stars and worlds. This is the basis for the science of Astrology.

It should be noted, however, that the Light is an influence, not a deciding factor. Each individual still has free will to respond to the circumstances of their lives in the ways that they choose.

A Downward Spiral and the Rescue

In this way, the influences of this Solar System are a combination of the actions, thoughts, and feelings of all the beings within it. You can understand why the Earth has had to be in quarantine for so long. It was capable of polluting the Universe. And even while quarantined, so to speak, from other planets in the Solar System, it was capable of having an effect on them. The nature of the quarantine was, shall we say, self-created. As the energies of the downward spiral of involution continued, Earth fell out of control. Earth was on a collision course for self-destruction.

This was the point at which Sanat Kumara, the Planetary Logos of Venus, volunteered to hold the light for the Earth. He came with 144,000 volunteers from Venus until humanity was ready to hold the light itself.

Ultimately, many Beings acted to rescue the Earth. They volunteered to bring their own consciousness, their own Life and Light, to the collective momentum so that the dangerous spiral into oblivion could be corrected.

It is the collective thoughts, prayers, feelings and actions of humanity which determine what level of vibration, or Light, the planet can maintain.

At a certain density, Life cannot be sustained, and the planet will attempt to restructure itself (much like a body fighting off disease) so that the light level needed to sustain life can be maintained. Therefore, we have natural cataclysms, tornadoes, etc. However, it was possible, even if mankind did not destroy itself, that the planet, in her attempt to cleanse herself, would actually self-destruct during the intensive bombardment with the Cosmic energies reaching the planet at this Cosmic moment.

Planetary Self-Destruction Has Been Averted.

We are so grateful to assure you that this scenario has definitely been averted, as have the ones requiring massive land convulsions. However, it is still necessary for the Earth to restructure herself in order to create the new pattern of Divine Harmonic in alignment with the new energies which are daily accelerating on the planet.

There will be a New Age of Love and Wisdom in which each being lives with great joy and prosperity upon the planet. It will surprise you how quickly the changes come. The change in consciousness will be in the twinkling of an eye. The change from poverty and lack to abundance and joy will take a bit longer as humanity must put its own hands to the plowshares for this transformation to take place.

As sharing and joyful community become the norm, there will be further shifts in understanding and in the expression of creativity, love and unity never before realized on this planet. Not even previous Golden Ages were able to achieve what lies in Earth's future.

I would point out at this time that the lives of the Great Avatars, Gautama Buddha and Jesus the Christ, created the pivotal energy that this planet needed in order to prepare for the present days of Cosmic change. Their lives were so radiant that millions were drawn to follow their teachings; and slowly the numbers of those capable of sustaining the Light grew.

There was a tremendous momentum in the other direction and negative forces strove mightily to prevent this change. Over the succeeding 2,500 years, an increasing number of lightworkers were adding their own momentum for the Light to the Earth's drama.

Opening of the Cosmic Gates

At the time of the Harmonic Convergence, there was the first in a series of Cosmic Gates which opened to allow an influx of light onto the planet. As each "gate" opened, higher levels of Cosmic Light, which formerly had not been able to reach the planet, vibrating at levels of greater Love than had been experienced for thousands of years, poured onto the planet. This was something destined to happen. These Cosmic Gates are part of God's plan built into the design and relationships of the stars.

Mankind's preparation for this time enabled enough souls to respond by accepting and correctly using these energies to allow themselves to receive even higher levels of Light. Many responded to the subtle increments that were occurring by improving their lives. People were striving to be more loving, to communicate better. Many were overcoming and releasing addictive behaviors that had been adding to the general density. They became part of the solution rather than part of the problem.

People were taking greater and greater responsibility for their actions. Some did not respond so well. There were outbreaks of wars and racial and national tensions as well. Earthquakes increased and so did strange changes in the planetary weather patterns.

The Awakening of the Lightworkers

Gradually, however, the changes for the better began to be

seen and felt. As the vibrational rate of the planet continued to increase, a new phenomenon had begun: the Awakening of the Lightworkers.

In 1991, Solara introduced the world to the 11:11 opening of the Cosmic Gateway. Many who were drawn to her teachings, began to realize that they were here with a Divine mission. They were Lightworkers here to assist in the cosmic Birthing of Planet Earth. Many began noticing their clocks at 11:11 AM and PM. Many synchronicities occurred triggering internal alarms to awaken.

Who were these Lightworkers? Many began to realize that they were volunteers from the Angelic kingdom. As these Angels in bodies began to reconnect with their true origins and with the Light, Love and Wisdom that was their true nature, they were able more consciously to shower their gifts of love, hope, wisdom, peace, beauty, and joy on their families, their neighbors, friends, and indeed to the whole planet.

Some of the awakening Lightworkers remembered recent lifetimes connected with other star systems like the Pleiades, Arcturus, and Sirius, and began connecting with the Lightships that were part of a vast Armada of loving helpers here to give whatever assistance they could within the limits of Divine Fiat.

That Fiat, or requirement, was that in order for the Higher Order of Beings to give assistance, someone in human form must ask for that help. This has always been true, but there is a tremendous amount of assistance available right now.

As the years continued to roll by, great changes were sweeping the Earth. The Berlin Wall came down. The Soviets released their stranglehold on their satellite countries, and life began to breathe back into Eastern Europe. Much damage had been done, much that had been brutally repressed under communism, now was coming up again. This time the pain must be addressed, and we must find the ways to heal the centuries of pain that are being expressed in seemingly endless wars.

The Resurrection of Planet Earth

The more people who awakened from the nightmare of hatred and isolation, of fear and separation, the easier it became to love, to forgive, and to give thanks. These are the tools that the Lightworkers are using everywhere to heal and to bless and to participate in the Resurrection of Planet Earth. These are the tools, taught by all the great Teachers, which reverse the involutionary trend into oblivion. These are the tools which lift the spirit, lift the consciousness, lift the heart, lift the planet back onto the return path to God.

It Becomes Easier to Love,
to Forgive, to Give Thanks.

But there were more awakenings to come. Many who had been counted as saints in previous centuries were awakening in the human forms that they had chosen for these times. There were Avatars, Divine Beings incarnated in human form, awakening in and through those who had chosen to be born at this time to give this service: Quan Yin, Krishna, Mother Mary, Shiva, Isis, and the long-awaited second coming of the Christ and the Buddha.

As well, due to the tremendous spiritual potency of these days, others in the process of healing, clearing and doing their spiritual work were merging with these Divine Beings. Gods and Goddesses were being reborn around the Earth in full harmony, love, and cooperation with their human partners. Heaven and Earth were merging. A New Heaven and a New Earth were emerging.

In esoteric literature, Jesus was understood to have united fully with the Cosmic Christ presence during his lifetime.

Many understand these present times to be the "end of days" spoken of in the scriptures. Many await the second coming. Preceding this is a time of great testing. In Biblical terms, it is a time of the separation of the "sheep" from the "goats." Jesus' teachings and those of other great spiritual teachers and traditions have shown what we must do. We are being called to live the highest and the best lives we can—to be examples to our brothers and sisters and to share what we have.

Those who share find that more is being given to them. Those who give love are finding love expanding in their lives. Those who serve are finding new opportunities to serve opening to them with ever richer rewards in all areas of their lives.

We are being tested daily around issues of money, trust, love, compassion, understanding, judgment, and on and on. We are being given these opportunities because the Earth is returning to a state comparable to that which existed in the Garden of Eden. We will know that all of our needs are taken care of perfectly. From this knowing and trusting, we will be able to share with those in need. We will trust our instincts and our guidance. Right action will become natural and effortless as our lives are aligned more and more for the highest good of all.

Planetary Mirrors

At this time we are confronting all of our personal demons. We are taking long hard looks at ourselves, both individually and collectively. O.J. Simpson's trial was the trial of all of us. There were daily news reports for over a year, and it seemed to be on everyone's mind constantly. Now, of course, we can barely remember it.

Notice now, in retrospect, that the judge, the jury, the attorneys, the press and the public were on trial as well. The questions were, "What is ethical? What is moral? What are we as a society choosing? What part of ourselves do we deny or judge when we think this case is about someone else? How is this a mirror for all of us?"

More recently, we have the experience of September 11, 2001. How is this a mirror for each of us? What do we fear? What do we resist? What do we honor and admire?

Indeed, we are looking at ourselves very deeply at this time. We are looking at the nature of the choices and decisions that have shaped our lives. We are deciding if these are decisions which are still what we want. Many of us have begun dealing with the issues of our early childhood.

The Inner Child is something people are becoming pretty aware of now. We are, for the most part, healing ourselves. We are choosing more wisely, finding new and healthier ways of relating to our friends and families and to our lives. We are choosing more love—for ourselves, for one another, for the Earth.

It had been thought that there would be many people unable to deal with the increases in Light and that many would choose to die because conditions became too difficult. In 1994, it was reported that so many had chosen to stay and to deal with their issues that the massive loss of life that had been anticipated was not going to happen.

It was, in fact, due to these very, individual choices all over the planet, that the final horrible holocaust that had been predicted was averted. That change was announced in 1989. By 1995, there had been plenty of upheaval which continued to the end of the century. Y2K was the big question in everyone's mind. Would all of our systems collapse? With great relief we greeted the New Millennium to find all was well.

Change is, however, still in everyone's life. The Light levels continue to increase, and we continue to be confronted with those patterns and choices from the past which never worked very well and now *really* don't work. We are needing as never before the tools of transformation.

In order to make the transformation into Light that is called for at this time, we must requalify more than 50% of all the energy that we have ever misqualified in any lifetime. (The rest is constantly corrected through an act of Divine Grace and Forgiveness.) This means that all of our problems at this time are the reflection of those patterns of misqualified energy striving to be corrected. In order to Ascend, we must requalify every iota of energy ever misqualified in every lifetime.

Our planet is scheduled to ascend into the fifth dimension. This dimension is also known as Christ Consciousness. Thus, our planet is destined to be a Christed planet. This means that all on it must be operating at at that level of consciousness and love, or beyond, or it would be too painful to remain. This is a vibratory frequency as well as a state of awareness.

Author's comment: As of 1998, the alignment with the Fifth Dimension was reported as accomplished by various authors. From today's perspective, we would say that while the fifth dimension is clearly anchored on Earth, there is still the tendency to drift back into the more limited thinking and perspectives of the third dimension. Continue to remind yourself that remaining established in fifth dimensional consciousness will be the greatest help in maintaining right thought and choosing right action in the days to come. The errors and confusions of the third dimension will not be sustained, however, we are still in the transition period and its experiences are still affecting you.

There has been a clear shifting in the trajectory that Earth was on twice in the last ten years. The first occurred when Clinton was elected. Despite a great deal of confusion and disillusionment during that administration, the general mood of the country was strong. Our economy was strong and there was a focus on more care for the environment and respect for human rights.

After George Bush took office in 2001, a second shift in trajectory happened. There was a reversal of what many viewed as progress made during the Clinton administration. This may have created some reversals. It does coincide with the onset of the Tribulation.

We remind our readers that following any Initiation or Ascension, there is a period before moving fully into the completion of one cycle to the beginning of the next when it is possible to lose the attainment, or to fall back energetically.

In 2001, this is what happened. Our world slipped backward. Always, though, this is in order to lay a more firm foundation and regain what was lost. The events of September 11th were a reflection of this loss. In similar circumstances, an individual might have to become seriously ill. Many who battle illness have found that it carried the seed of a great lesson for them, and they are grateful.

I remind each of you who may be resisting these words, we are all part of One Being. If there is war, aggression, even terrorism in the world, in some way the seed, at least, is in each one of us.

To root out terrorism and other acts of negativity and aggression correctly, we must each look within ourselves to address that anger, that rage, that pain within ourselves.

Denial and rejection merely prolong the problem. Life brings these reflections to us so we may see ourselves more clearly. Look within yourself. Identify that which requires healing and take responsibility for those things within yourself that must be corrected.

Bottling up rage leads to disease both in individuals and in society. Merely returning aggression with aggression does not heal—it perpetuates. It is interesting to see the struggle in society to both attack and stop the terrorists and to help those who are bearing the brunt of war, hatred and danger in their daily lives.

It is a measure of the courage and compassion of the American people that the predominant response was one of reaching out in service and self-sacrifice to help both at home and abroad.

Yes, those who endanger others must be stopped as well—but, we must be careful not to place so much attention on terrorists that we become that which we have focused upon. Or, as Pogo once so wisely stated, "we have met the enemy, and he is us."

ഔ൨൵

In order for the planet to maintain the frequency of Ascension in this next cycle, we must continue to requalify the vast accumulation from all previous civilizations of negatively qualified energy at the physical, emotional, mental and etheric levels, and we must keep clearing that which is being released during this very intense time.

As we enter the New Millennium, the question is often raised, "Now that we have ascended the planet, why aren't things any easier?" It is because, beloved ones, in your great love and compassion, you have insisted that as many as possible be brought along with you. They are daily facing mighty challenges and are being given every assistance. *(See new update on page 121.)*

For those of you who are wishing that things could be a little easier for you, we offer the following suggestions.

First, if you have been facing financial challenges in attempting to focus completely on your New Age activities, begin now to see how they might be incorporated as valuable for all humanity, not just the "Lightworkers." You will notice that many mainstream stores (grocery, book and drugstores for example) now include many health, holistic and New Age products.

Health care, churches, businesses and corporations are now more ready than ever to open to New Age proposals, as long as they can see their worth in their own terms. This means that there are many opportunities opening to you now in areas that seemed closed for many years. It is time to end the separation between the old and the new. Let there be a healing and rebirth for all.

Second, continue to do your clearing work, as ever deeper levels of self are ready to be healed now. Remember to ask the Angels to bring you whatever assistance you might need.

Third, continue to remember that all are your sisters and brothers; some just haven't remembered it yet. You do not need to force your beliefs or your ways on anyone else. You do not need to hide or bury them either. You will know that you are in the right place, doing the right thing, when you feel safe, nurtured, welcomed and loved. Yes, you still have room for growth, and you are perfect as you are, as well. Love yourself now.

For those who have been longing for community, know that all is moving forward toward that perfect accomplishment. Hold that thought in your mind as you make your choices and act in the world. Remember the Native American idea of making sure that something was good for seven generations. When your goals and principles are behind every choice, all will surely lead to the outcome you desire.

For those who have been longing for the perfect Divine partner, know that that too is moving toward its perfect outcome. God knows what is in your heart and it is His/Her Loving Will that it be accomplished.

(Update: We are still operating with a mix of dimensions and I refer you to the 9D Council Update of July 26, 2001 received by Jelaila Starr for the Nibiruan Council. See www. nibiruancouncil.com/html/july2001update.html.

In summary, we are directed to address the distancing

that is now present between those who focus primarily in the third dimension and those operating from the fourth and fifth dimensions. We are urged to give more direct teaching and assistance to those still stuck in the third dimensional paradigm. We would mention that this article also speaks directly to the star seeds about their mission.)

There is a further update that I feel must be added here. In September, 2002, I received an email sent around the world by spiritual teacher Patricia Cota Robles. She was reporting on the events of her annual celebration held this year in Washington, D.C. Each year she and those attending participate in much planetary healing work. This year during their prayers, they were working with the souls of those who have been known as "laggards"—ones who have not made the planetary Ascension in other systems and were brought to Earth for another chance.

For some years now, those with the inner awareness to perceive such things have felt that there was a distinct possibility that many of these would not come along with the planet and in fact that there might even end up being two Earths—one that Ascended and one that did not.

At this particular event, these souls committed to do whatever work was required of them to heal and to be raised up with the rest of humanity. There will be only one planet. When this occurred, you might have noticed it yourself, for a mighty change occurred at that moment. I know several people whose plans were dramatically stopped and then changed at that time.

This was a significant event in Earth's history and it has affected the future. For more information see her website: www.1spirit.com/eraofpeace.

In October, 2002, we have also been informed that the Earth has entered the fifth Dimension. You may have been noticing more instant manifestations, not all of them what you had hoped. *Remember to be even more cautious in your spoken word. Things are definitely happening faster and faster.*

Many awaited December 12 - 21, 2012 as the end of the Mayan calendar and perhaps the end of the known world. Indeed, ever-increasing floods of light entered our atmosphere. Highly unusual astrological alignments of the sun, moon and planets were noted. Many noticed that they were given new "asskgnments". Still more were finding their lives shifted and changed through loss of familiar jobs, forclosure on their homes or sudden health crises. Gratitude and awareness are the keys now. Choose that which brings you joy.

Many authors are presenting material at this time on different facets of what we are referring to here. Their information may be a little behind or a little ahead of what we are explaining. Please remember that what is being presented in these asides is an in-the-moment assessment of what is happening. There are still so many choices of such magnitude being made that the future is less and less predictable.

Why do some prophecies appear to be so accurate and others so variable? It is not because God is speaking to one and not the other. Rather, certain prophecies of that which God knows to be true are intended to be expressed for a variety of reasons. For example, one might be to offer hope, another forewarning.

Those prophecies or predictions which are of a more variable nature also have reason for being expressed. It is perhaps even more important to be aware of possible futures, so that we might act in such a way as to cooperate with our outer concerns and our inner awareness and find the Highest possible action that we can take toward a future that we would actually prefer.

Choose that which brings you Joy.

Chapter Ten

Initiations - Human and Solar

Lord Jesus/Sunanda speaks:

Beloveds, I Am Sunanda,

I this chapter we are going to be introducing to you the concepts of Soul, Oversoul or Higher Self, and levels of Consciousness. We will be attempting, by means which are linear and limited in nature, to describe that which is non-linear and unlimited.

We are going to describe to you your own Essence—your own Divinity—and, to some extent, the ways in which you yourself are One with All That Is. This concept of Oneness has seemed like a mental construct, one that you couldn't really grasp. We intend by presenting this model to you, to give you something, which by expanding your understanding of the general principles, can allow you to understand God and your relationship within that Allness a little more deeply and more personally, to understand that you are God.

Let us start by examining the three-dimensional reality of which you are aware. You have been introduced to the three dimensions as height, length and depth. These in fact, are descriptions of the first dimension—the Physical. Attempts to construct models of other dimensions from this perspective are therefore doomed to error. A faulty premise leads to faulty conclusions.

You are quite aware of the second dimension, the Emotional plane, sometimes called the astral plane. It is the field of your emotions and feelings.

The third is the Mental plane. Here you experience thoughts, ideas, memories and various mental constructs.

Each dimensional reality exists in a vibrational frequency band. Physical reality—what you can see, hear, smell, taste and touch is what science has limited itself to measuring. And because it has not been able to design tools which can measure or interact with the higher frequency bands, it often attempts to deny their existence.

We will be as clear as we can be here. Perhaps some enterprising scientists will be inspired to explore the world a little differently and thereby be able to construct some heretofore "impossible" gadgets for your use and enjoyment. These are the principles that will allow interstellar and interspecies communication, space travel and some marvels of transport and communication as well as labor saving devices at home.

The Physical band is the densest and slowest. Just as certain gases are heavier than others and only rise to certain levels in the atmosphere, so the physical frequency band only exists within a certain range.

The second or Emotional frequency band interpenetrates the physical and extends somewhat beyond it.

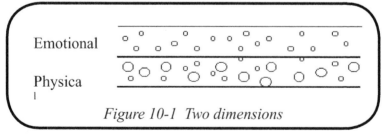

Figure 10-1 Two dimensions

In our image *(Figure 10-1)*, we represent the physical by the large particles and the emotional by the medium size particles, which extend beyond the range of the physical, but also completely penetrate the physical. Just as physics sometimes defines light as a wave and sometimes as a particle, so too, these vibrational patterns might be viewed in the same way.

The third dimension band is the Mental. It also exists at a higher frequency and with still smaller particles. These mental energies also interpenetrate the previous bands and extend a little beyond. These higher frequencies are represented by the very small dots in the diagram *(Figure 10-2)*.

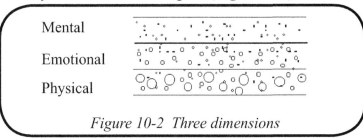

Mental

Emotional

Physical

Figure 10-2 Three dimensions

Much as air is very dense at low altitudes and very thin and fine at higher altitudes, thoughts are also both dense and fine. The higher altitudes of the mental carry only higher thoughts. And the higher thoughts also can penetrate into the denser planes. Thus, Dante and Michelangelo and Leonardo DaVinci brought their inspired ideas to earth.

We will now extend these principles of higher and higher frequency bands into the next several dimensional realities. We point out to you that the terms that are used here are not exactly the same as are used in Alice Bailey or various sacred texts, such as the Hindu scriptures. The ideas and the concepts are the same; the names are different. As there are so many different systems, we choose one where the names have a certain degree of familiarity.

The system which we will be describing is composed of seven levels (or vibrational frequencies) of consciousness.

These seven vibrational levels correspond to the seven stages of the initiatory journey described by Djwal Khul through author Alice Bailey in the books *Initiations Human and Solar* and *The Rays and the Initiations*.

As you prepare yourself for discipleship and eventual Mastery, you begin to move from the unawakened or unenlightened state of consciousness to the Awakened or Enlightened state. As you take each initiation, your consciousness becomes sensitive to the vibratory patterns of the next higher frequency. You move from a limited awareness to a more expanded state. You become aware of levels of knowing and wisdom not previously accessible to you, and you have a greater ability to give and receive Love.

There are stages of awareness, or levels of Initiation, that you pass through. We are going to speak of this from the perspective of the human who is taking the first steps.

The Human Rounds of Evolution

In the book, *Initiation,* author Elizabeth Haich describes the preliminary stages prior to Initiation *(See particularly pages 132-134 in her book.)*:

Seven years of service-oriented work while consciously unaware of the other realms.

A testing or probationary stage of trial. You ask yourself, "Are you sure you want to do this?" You let go of attachments. This was exemplified by the apostles who let go of their previous careers to follow Jesus.

The first Initiation marks the passing of certain tests of mastery over the physical plane and completion of the probationary period. Letting go of those beliefs and attachments related to issues of employment, health, housing, food, exercise are all prominent. Actual physical challenges may also be involved.

The second Initiation marks the meeting of challenges of emotional issues such as overcoming fears, resentment, jealousy, and so forth. Usually only one issue or configuration of issues is dealt with at a time.

The third Initiation marks the mastery over issues of a

mental nature. It is a time of re-examining beliefs and values, of clearing and healing conscious and subconscious patterns, and aligning with the higher mind.

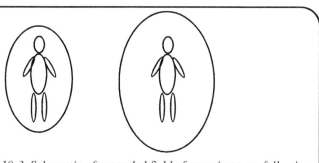

Figure 10-3 Schematic of expanded field of consciousness following an initiation.

The fourth Initiation marks the movement into the higher realms. It is also called the Crucifixion or Great Renunciation. It is marked by sacrifice, suffering, and is often perceived as strenuous, hard and painful.

Djwal Khul describes it this way:

"He has laid all, even his perfected personality, upon the altar of sacrifice, and stands bereft of all. All is re-nounced: friends, money, reputation, character, standing in the world, family and even life itself." (from Alice Bailey's book, *"Initiation - Human and Solar,"* p.89)

This is quickly followed by the Fifth Initiation, the Resurrection, attaining Christ Consciousness.

When Jesus said, "none can come to the Father except through me," (John 14:6), He referred to the need to unify with one's own Christ Self (the fifth Initiation) in order to proceed to the next step or union with the I AM.

The sixth Initiation is the Ascension—the uniting with The Individualized God Self—God as Father, God as Mother—the I AM Presence. This includes the opportunity to stay on Earth and serve the Divine Plan (the Boddhisatva choice) or to go on to other service. *(You might wish to reread this several times, or to sit with it and contemplate its meaning.)*

The seventh Initiation is a time of great awareness and connection with the Divine with All that Is and a time for extreme caution in one's choices and actions. It may include the loss of all that has gone before and the reclaiming of it, either literally or just the letting go of all attachment.

Here one may "lose" one's prior attainment and be faced with either reclaiming the attainment and clearing and correcting the error that precipitated the loss or one may be faced with illness if no correction is made.

However, one completes this step, one then moves to the next level of complexity returning to the Physcial level in a higher cycle and the Initiations continue.

Seventh	- All That Is - Celestial
Sixth	- I Am—the Mother-Father Principle
Fifth	- Christ
Fourth	- Etheric
Third	- Mental
Second	- Emotional or Astral
First	- Physical

Figure 10-4: Seven planes of Consciousness of the Human Rounds of Initiation/Evolution.

Once the soul has achieved a certain level of consciousness and spiritual attainment, the physical body cannot remain in good health at lower levels. If one has "fallen backwards" either a little or a lot, it is imperative to identify the error and correct it. These errors are those thoughts, words or actions which can no longer be sustained at the new vibrational frequency.

These days we are constantly urged to move forward to

greater and greater achievements; not for ourselves, not for ego or personal satisfaction, but because humanity's need is so great. As we are lifted up, all life is lifted up with us. These days of rapid acceleration demand our highest and truest efforts.

As we are lifted up all life is lifted up.

The seventh Initiation also marks the opportunity for a return to the physical for the next cycle of seven. If one has left the physical body behind through death or taken it along into the other dimensions, there may be an extended phase before a return to the physical plane through birth or other extremely rare incarnational methods. For example, Great Divine Beings might merge with the consciousness of an Initiate or chela (student) in the course of their Celestial Expressions through the physical plane.

At this time, it is necessary to attain more than 50 percent level of mastery to take the next Initiation. The remainder of the attainment is given as a Divine Dispensation, according to Patricia Cota Robles, to meet the needs of these times. It does mean that there is still some time needed for complete alignment with the new levels of energy and awareness after an Initiation. This pattern then repeats itself at a higher level of complexity.

Seven sets of seven Initiations complete the human rounds of Evolution. Each of these Initiations represents progress through various subplanes of still higher cycles of Initiation and mastery. As one progresses through these stages, the degree of mastery that must be demonstrated is expanded to include greater and greater level of detail. For example, one man might learn to run a lathe, another to supervise the entire shop and a third to run the company. All of these might be tasks of mastery of different levels of complexity on the physical plane. ,

None of these tasks denote spiritual mastery, but each might be a part of the work of a spiritual master dealing with life on the physical plane. Equally, it might be the task to let go of any particular job, no matter how glamorous, well-paid, or difficult.

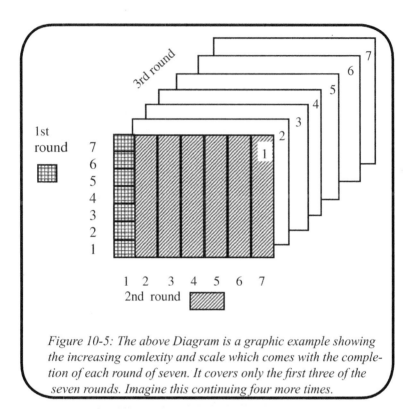

Figure 10-5: The above Diagram is a graphic example showing the increasing comlexity and scale which comes with the completion of each round of seven. It covers only the first three of the seven rounds. Imagine this continuing four more times.

The diagram in Figure 10-5 represents the increasing levels of complexity (*represented by the larger size*) demanded as one passes through the various cycles or rounds of initiation.

In the first round or set of seven Initiations, each step is of a more limited nature (*represented by small squares in figure 10-5*). The complete set of seven then becomes the first unit of a larger set of seven (*rectangles with diagonal slashes*).

Then this complete set, becomes the first unit of a still larger set of seven (larger squares). This repeats seven times (*only three are represented in Figure 10-5*).

So, there are seven sets of seven Initiations in the human rounds of evolution. And there are seven levels of Ascension, one in each of the seven rounds.

Ascension is union with Mother/Father God -- the individualized I Am Presence. (The I Am is One with all other individualized I Am Presences.) Each succeeding Ascension experience marks a deeper union with the I Am Presence. At some point in this unification process, the I Am Presence will merge with the Initiate, and she or he will become an embodiment of the Higher Self, as still vaster Cosmic cycles of Initiation, growth and learning proceed. This process continues as one ascends through the levels of the Angelic cycles, and greater and greater aspects of the I Am merge into form.

Angelic (or Solar) Rounds of Evolution

Upon completion of the seven sets of seven, one is finished with the human rounds of evolution and begins on the Angelic (or Solar) rounds which include 12 sets of 12 steps, 12^{12} or 12 x 12 x 12 x 12 x 12 x 12 x 12 x 12 x 12 x 12 x 12 x 12. Here the expansion occurs as six additional steps within the levels of the I Am Presence.

These additional levels include the planetary Buddha, three levels of the Cosmic Void/Divine Mother (see page 136 for more details on the Void), the Cosmic Christ, Cosmic Buddha and the Cosmic Mother. These are all distinct levels of consciousness. The thirteenth level is a point of completion of the cycle, bathing in the Infinite Source and perhaps receiving new encodements for the next cycle. At this time in history, one quickly moves into the next larger cycle , from the physical level onward.

In Angelic cycles one begins to interact with those who are Angels in form, Gods and Goddesses in form, Christs and Buddhas in form, Avatars in form. You may be surprised to find yourself meeting Jesus expressing through a number of individuals or Mother Mary, Quan Yin and many other well known Divine Beings. For example, during his incarnation, Krishna was said to be in over 10,000 bodies.

13th - All that Is - Celestial
12th* - Cosmic Mother
11th* - Cosmic Buddha
10th* - Cosmic Christ
 9th*† - Cosmic Void - Center of Perfect Peace
 8th*† - Cosmic Void - the Tao - the Holy Spirit
 7th*† - Cosmic Void - Emptiness - All potential
 6th*- Planetary Buddha
 5th - Planetary Christ
 4th - Etheric
 3rd - Mental
 2nd - Emotional or Astral
 1st - Physical
  (* All within the I Am Presence.)
  († All levels of the Divine Mother)

*Figure 10-6   Twelve + one planes of Consciousness
of the Angelic or Solar Rounds of Initiation*

Through most of our recorded history, this has been a far more infrequent process. At this time, however, due to the confluence of Vast Cosmic Cycles, there are unprecedented opportunities for growth at these Cosmic levels. And many thousands of incarnate Divine Beings are now here on Earth participating in this vast Cosmic interplay.

Cycles of time are converging at this point in human evolution.

We have reached

the end of a decade: 1990s

the end of a century: 1900s

the end of a millennium: 1000s

the end of an Astrological Age;

the Piscean becomes the Aquarian: (2,000+ years)

the end of a Mayan Calendar: (12,000+ years)

We approach the end of a Yuga or age:
(186,000+ years) (Kali Yuga)
There are vast planetary, solar, galactic and universal Initiations happening now, and still to come. See *Pillar of Celestial Fire* by Robert Cox for an excellent explanation of the cycles of Cosmic Time.

Earth's Evolution

The Earth has reached her own point of evolution. You will see that many national and racial groups have passed through their own Crucifixion Initiation. The Irish, the Jews, the Native Americans, the Tibetans, all of Europe, South Africans, the Cambodians, the Chinese, the Japanese, the Rwandans, the Hawaiian people, the Iraqi and the Afghanistani people to name a few. The Earth herself will pass through this phase, so that what has been predicted as Armageddon has been experienced by all.

And yet, due to the work by masses of humanity, the Earth has Ascended.

(Author's note 1997: As I looked at what was still to come I saw that there are veils over the details because it depends on the individual and collective efforts of all of humanity, from the most to the least evolved.

We can say that the more terrible predictions and prophecies have indeed been averted—some at the eleventh hour.)

Initiation

An Initiation as here described is a permanent, upward shift in the vibrational frequency of the body, based on lessons completed, tasks accomplished and love expressed. This is experienced as more Light at the atomic and cellular level and throughout the body, thus the term "enlightenment." One might even experience a slight burning sensation within the

The Cosmic Void

(Given to Mikaelah Cordeo by Mother Mary in 1991.)

All three levels of the Void are a part of the Consciousness of the Divine Mother. The first level of the Cosmic Void is experienced as a great emptiness. For some, this can be a very frightening experience. For others, there is no judgment. (In your daily life, you might feel confused, directionless or lost.)

As you allow your consciousness to move to the next level, you might imagine you are taking a microscope to a higher level of magnification.

At the second level, you will perceive myriad minute particles of potential matter moving randomly within what was previously perceived as empty space. Within the randomness, you will be able to perceive an array of particles that appears as a river or great flow. This is the flow created by all the choices within creation as potential is actualized. It is the Tao—the Way.

Again increasing your perceptual magnification, you can move to the third level. Move your conscious awareness within the flow of the Tao. Here you will find at the very center the place of Perfect Peace. Around the center you might experience the flow as a whirlwind. This whirlwind and its center of stillness may also be thought of as the breath of the Holy Spirit.

When you are in the center, all is still and peaceful. Indeed, from that place of stillness you draw to you all that is perfect for you. It is from this place that you can manifest what you need perfectly. Only your fears will interfere. On the other hand, away from the center you will experience the whirlwind. It can feel chaotic and as though you are tossed and turned by circumstance. You are relentlessly pushed back to the center.

Allowing yourself to experience these levels will take you into a new understanding of creating your reality cells, as that which remains to be purified at this new level is literally "burned off" by the higher vibratory action.

Often there is the experience of stepping through a doorway into a vast field of Light which is so bright it may be days or weeks before the inner sight adjusts enough to "see" what is there.

Following an initiation of the Light, one will experience greater ability to give and receive Love—as though the Chalice of the Self has expanded—and there is greater access to Wisdom. Certain thoughts, ideas, and understandings will be available which were not accessible before. (Refer to the earlier model of the different sized particles in the different dimensional realities.) You have gained access to the next higher frequency band, and that information is now accessible to your conscious mind. It may have been all around you, but you could not relate to it or understand it. Now, your physical, emotional and mental vehicle is altered, and you can interpret it.

There are also Initiations of sound, the breath or wind, and other choices which have application in various lives. In the first Ramtha book, he described his initiation by the wind.

It is also true that certain thoughts, ideas and behaviors which cannot co-exist in the new levels of Light may come up to be recognized, healed, purified and released.

It is helpful and very important to consciously release all that no longer serves you at the new level of consciousness. Focus on releasing from the physical, emotional, mental and higher bodies all that no longer serves you. Clear with Violet Flame and refill the cleared space with Gold or White Light.

If this is not recognized, we point out to you that it is possible to lose one or more levels of attainment through attachment to old patterns of thought and behavior that are not in harmony with the new standards. If this is the case, it is an opportunity to regroup, build your foundation more firmly, and move forward again. Once this process is started, it can lead to serious physical damage to revert to lower levels and not clear whatever is needed in order to move on. The events of September 11, 2001 were a terrible example of this on a planetary scale.

This does not happen often, but it can, and everyone should be aware of this. It is best to remember that this is not a punishment, nor is it Divine Will that you be brought low; rather, it is a consequence of your choices. Choosing differently will enable you to move forward again. This is sometimes referred to as "walking the razor's edge." There is not much room for sloppy thinking as you progress.

We would point out to you that we take initiations not just as individuals, but as groups both large and small, and sometimes as the whole of humanity. The most recent events that were truly experienced world wide were the death of Princess Diana and the cataclysmic acts on September 11th, 2001.

The following section is an adaptation of an article by Mikaelah Cordeo called "Crossing the Abyss," published in Spring, 1993, in the publication, "COR Connections."

Crossing the Abyss

There are many Lightworkers who have given up all ties to their former lives—ties that were based on the old programs of hard work, co-dependency and various other culturally imposed expectations and values. They are learning to trust God for their daily needs. They are learning to love and trust each other. They are learning to live every day in God Consciousness, Christ Consciousness. They are learning to trust and honor their physical bodies while surrendering to the guidance of the Spirit within.

We are learning that abundance comes in many forms, not just money or material prosperity. We are learning to recognize the hand of God in our lives and to *give thanks in all things.* We are also learning to heal our issues around money and to accept it and other forms of material prosperity as part of a growing sense of worthiness.

It seems that we are surviving with no visible means of support. I call this crossing the abyss. This is part of the experience of the Cosmic Void. Within the void one experiences the subatomic particles that are the building blocks of form, the particles of all potential reality. By becoming clear in this awareness, one can gain the confidence of the ability to manifest one's reality in full alignment with the flow of life. At the center of the Void one can find the place of perfect Peace, the center of Stillness. Here is found a new perspective for seeing life and finding the Way.

I came to realize that once we have crossed this seeming abyss, we end up back in the Garden of Eden—that is, in a state of consciousness in which we have total trust in the Truth that we are always Divinely guided and protected, that all that we need is provided for us.

When we learn to step out of our own way, to live in joyous expectation and trust, we can see the gifts that God/Goddess is always sending to us. When we believe how deeply we are loved, we can see ourselves as worthy of these gifts and allow ourselves to receive them.

There is a wave of new awakenings crossing the planet with our entrance into the Millennium. This is a reminder that others have walked this way before. Did you see the movie in which Indiana Jones stepped in faith from the edge of the cliff into the abyss and the path appeared bneath his feet?

Know that whatever the seeming appearances of your life, you are cared for. The path is revealed as it is needed, sometimes only one step at a time

Involution or Evolution

The Cosmic forces of Involution and Evolution loom large

in your lives today. To state it simply, the forces of involution bring your energy down. These include the negative patterns, the sins of the Bible: attitudes such as jealousy, resentment, criticism and complaining, as well as the more obvious behaviors of lying, greed, gluttony, stealing, murder, rape, etc.

Those choices which are evolutionary raise your energy and lead to further Initiations, the growth and maturation of your soul. Choices such as forgiveness, gratitude, joy, laughter, service, sharing, devotion, sacred or devotional music and prayer—the virtues—are evolutionary.

Where Are We Going?

What can you do now? Work on yourself. Examine your beliefs, your thoughts, your words, your deeds. Pray, meditate, fast as feels timely or appropriate. Begin to look at your brothers and sisters on this planet with the eyes of the Christ and the compassion of the Buddha. Look with love and compassion on one another.

The largest step still to be taken is a collective one for all humanity. It is a Group Initiation, if you will. Groups that have been separate will join together. Religions will choose to honor one another. Out of this will come a World Day of Praising God—with prayer, meditation, fasting—a celebration of worship of the Divinity that is God in everyone and everything. This will be a day celebrated by everyone, all over the planet.

This day of Unification across the racial, national and religious boundaries will mark the completion of the old cycles of death and rebirth; and it will mark the beginning of a new cycle of the manifestation of a New Heaven and a New Earth.

This day will mark the end of the Tribulation.

Chapter Eleven

The Realignment Process

Beloved, I Am Sunanda. I Am your Sun.

We ask that you begin with a 15 minute meditation. And then we will proceed. (I received these instructions before I began this chapter, I include it, as all are the Beloved, and meditation has value for you as well. MC)

You are, Beloved Ones, undergoing a time of tremendous testing and challenge. We fully understand the difficulties you face and the confusion that frequently feels overwhelming.

There are certain underlying forces at work in your lives at this time and we hope that these clarifications will enable you to better understand exactly what is happening and to move through these times with grace and ease.

Many of you have heard that you are entering a time where your double strands of DNA are being replaced with twelve (12) strands.

This is representative of the 12-dimensional vehicle of Solar Light with which you are being encoded. These strands are being built upon the inner dimensions. Each strand is linked to a different dimensional reality.

As you stabilize your physical-etheric vehicles on each of the twelve dimensions, the Living Template of Light is linked together.

Prior to this stabilization, what you see around you are multiple opportunities. Each of them has its point of harmony within various levels of your 12-fold auric field or they could not have been magnetized to you at all. However, and this is a big however, most of these opportunities are not in harmony with all of the layers of your field.

For centuries, your bodies were stable in three dimensional reality. Thus, you could live with the situations you drew to yourself. And you did, often for entire lifetimes, even when there were large distortions in the etheric patterns.

At this time, those etheric patterns are being aligned with the wholeness and perfection of your Divine Blueprint and the Divine Blueprint for the Earth. It is for this reason that there is this massive re-examination of long held beliefs and cultural norms and expectations.

Only those patterns that are in harmonic resonance with the Love Vibration will be able to remain stable here on Earth.

Nothing will escape this realignment process. Again we say to you: All the bonds that are less than Love are being broken.

All the Bonds that are less than Love are being Broken.

Thus, the monetary systems, food production, health care, the very nature of the family, government, friendships, work—everything is undergoing a massive realignment with that which is Real—that which is True.

With the simple question, *"Is it Love that draws me or keeps me in this circumstance?"* you can begin to find those points of true stability for yourself. Are you living, working, sharing your life because of guilt, greed or fear? These reasons will become less and less viable as the days go on.

You are more and more conscious of the sheer goodness that can be your experience if you just allow your conscious mind to listen to what is truly right for you.

What do you want? Ask yourself this question until you begin to look for the deeper values which underlie all the "wants" and desires of your life.

Do you want a vacation to Bermuda? Why? Is it to impress your friends, to let go of stress, to experience blue sky, warm water and serenity, to follow an inner prompting that has no obvious reason? Why?

Go deep, beloved ones. Go deep into your hearts and find the Truth of knowing that lies hidden there. Allow these last few years of transition to be times of learning to love yourself more deeply, to listen to yourself more clearly, to trust yourself more truly.

In this loving, listening, trusting process, there will be much need for discernment as well. Is there distortion being reflected back to you as you listen to that inner voice? Perhaps the wounded inner child is angry or wants to run away and hide.

When you find these old patterns based in fear and pain, call on your Angels for healing and assistance. Call on Beloved Jesus or Mother Mary to comfort, heal or protect you. Call on your Higher Self to help you find the right choices as you walk the labyrinths of these days. Ask the Holy Spirit to bring healing and clarity to your mind and your decisions.

We want to remind you, Beloved Ones, no matter how complex the labyrinth, nor how many twists and turns, it leads you unerringly to the center. There are no false directions.

Ask for the deities or Divine Beings with whom you most align in faith, love and trust to come and give you their assistance: Mother Mary, Jesus, Buddha, Mother Meera, Krishna, Buddha, Sai Baba, Jesus, Ganesha, Quan Yin, Divine Mother.

There have been many forms of Divinity expressing on Earth. Perhaps one was the biggest or the best. Perhaps all were expressions of the One.

Let your heart direct you here. God knows your heart and hears what you long for and need.

Allow yourself to see the gifts that are brought to you every moment so that you might know how deeply you are loved.

Exercise 11-1: Gratitude

To close this section we ask you to take a moment for this very simple exercise. Sit quietly and comfortably and close your eyes. Find ten things in your life for which you are grateful and say thank you. (If you find this difficult, it is all the more necessary.)

Any ten things—air, trees, happy memories, a smile, an opportunity to share your love, a flower, a safe and happy home, your eyes, health, good mind... whatever it is, say, "Thank you, God/Goddess, thank you." Don't elaborate. Keep this exercise simple and pure. What are you grateful for? State it and say thank you. If you wish to add, "Thank you for the love which is every day filling and surrounding me," please do. You may not have been noticing it, but nevertheless, it is true.

Now, beloved ones, think of ten things you want or need. Make a list if you wish. And say:

"Thank you God/Goddess/Higher Self for meeting my needs perfectly.

"Thank you for bringing the people, things and circumstances that are perfect for my growth and evolution, for my comfort, ease and health.

"Thank you for sacred relationships, for work that fulfills me, for mechanical objects that support and help me, for perfect health, for a healthy and safe environment.

"Thank you for Love, Wisdom and Power.
"Thank you for your miracles in my life.
"Thank you!"

Exercise 11-2: Intererdimensional Grounding

Because there is now the integration on Earth of many dimensional realities, not just the ones we have been used to, there is some integration work to be done. This exercise will align all the dimensional realities of your higher bodies so you will go forward with unified consciousness. We wish to acknowledge and thank Erik Berglund, a very talented and spirit-directed, musician and healer, who first passed it on to us.

You will find it particularly useful if you find you can't make up your mind about what to do. Perhaps one day you are seriously considering one alternative. The next an entirely different one seems to be best. This is often a reflection of the non-integration of your various dimensional bodies.

In one dimensional reality, one perspective may seem perfect. In another, an entirely different idea may seem best. When you have all the dimensions integrated, then you will find clarity of purpose most easily, as what is best for all aspects of you will be clear.

Stand and hold your arms out to the sides, palms up. Circling your arms up and backward, recite: "I am grounding my 13th body into my 12th body **now***!" (emphasize the now by making a strong downward movement with your arms.)*
Continue to circle your arms and say:
"I am grounding my 13th and 12th bodies into my 11th body **now***!" (Emphasize with hand; feel the integration.)*
"I am grounding my 13th, my 12th and my 11th bodies into my 10th body **now***!" (emphasis)*
"I am grounding my 13th , my 12th, my 11th and my

10th bodies into my 9th body
now!" *(emphasis)*

"*I am grounding my 13th, my 12th, my 11th, my 10th and my 9th bodies into my 8th body **now!**" (emphasis)*

"*I am grounding my 13th , my 12th , my 11th, my 10th, my 9th and my 8th bodies into my 7th body **now!**" (emphasis)*

"*I am grounding my 13th , my 12th , my 11th, my 10th, my 9th, my 8th and my 7th bodies into my 6th body **now!**" (emphasis)*

"*I am grounding my 13th , my 12th , my 11th, my 10th, my 9th, my 8th, my 7th body and my 6th body into my 5th body **now!**"(emphasis)*

"*I am grounding my 13th , my 12th , my 11th, my 10th, my 9th, my 8th, my 7th body, my 6th and my 5th bodies into my 4th body **now!**"(emphasis)*

"*I am grounding my 13th , my 12th , my 11th, my 10th, my 9th, my 8th, my 7th body, my 6th, my 5th and my 4th bodies into my 3rd body **now!**"(emphasis)*

"*I am grounding my 13th , my 12th , my 11th, my 10th, my 9th, my 8th, my 7th body, my 6th, my 5th, my 4th and my 3rd bodies into my 2nd body **now!**"(emphasis)*

"*I am grounding my 13th , my 12th , my 11th, my 10th, my 9th, my 8th, my 7th body, my 6th, my 5th, my 4th, my 3rd and my 2nd bodies into my 1st body **now!**"(emphasis)*

Feel the integration as you complete each cycle. Rest your arms as needed. Repeat regularly.

(Some are working with more levels and may include as many as feel right.)

Chapter Twelve

Reprogramming
the Subconscious Mind

Commander Ashtar speaks:

I Am Ashtar—the Commander in Chief (of the Interstellar fleet working with the Earth transition). Who are you?
You are the portion of the team which has chosen to incarnate
on Planet Earth to facilitate the historic change that is even
now under way. What does this mean to you?
*What has been the nature of the lessons here? (Here
Ashtar responds to Mikaelah as the scribe.) I respond to
your inner concerns about humanity and any errors which
you are judging in yourself. In particular, was free will a giant mistake? What will happen as we move into the collective
consciousness of unity? Are you now to be a simple, mindless
automaton, doing whatever you are told with no input?*
What was the point of all the lessons and the struggle
and the difficulty if the lesson was only that you don't need
to know anything or to think at all? Does this unification with
our Higher Self mean that you are to say yes to everything
you are told? Are you to have no ideas or input at all?
Well, hopefully, that is not the understanding that you
have gained. There is indeed purpose in your lessons of free
will, and not just what a bad idea it was in the first place.

The Collective Expression of Humanity

First of all, the idea of the collective expression of humanity is one that will incorporate the individuality of each of its parts. Secondly, the full expression of the Unified Spirit will be something we cannot imagine from the information presently available. Just as many cells come together and form an organ, many organs come together and form a living being. Now many individuals will come together and form the collective, unified Presence.

The collective form looks nothing like its parts, and yet each is an indispensable part. However, we are not yet finished with the individualization part, and we have no clear understanding of exactly when the unification will happen, possibly not for hundreds or thousands of years.

Free will is an excellent idea. It is a learning tool for all those who seek to understand the purpose of command— command of oneself and command of others when it is appropriate. There are times when each person must be a commander and when each must stand ready to be commanded. If one does not understand the pitfalls of failing to follow orders, or of following orders that are contrary to one's own sense of purpose and right and wrong, then one is not able to give commands which are likely to be of any use.

We are most concerned with the level of revolt that seems to be washing across the consciousness of the Lightworkers these days. Beloved ones, wake up! Do not allow yourselves to give in to the temptation of self pity accompanied by self aggrandizement.

Perhaps you *are* the cornerstone of the Divine Plan. As long as the human self is allowed to hold sway and to resist every prompting of the Higher Self and every urging of the Supreme and, indeed, to argue with the very facts of daily life, then we have nothing less than revolution in the ranks.

Yes, of course, you are worthy of all good things and deserve to have your every need taken care of. However, it is not in the best interests of your life, your soul growth or your life purpose to complain that every little thing is wrong with your life. Indeed, you will make yourself unfit for the job with these tactics. We wish to speak to you about the difference between involution and evolution.

Involution and Evolution

Up until the time of Lord Gautama Buddha and Lord Jesus the Christ, the people of Earth had been engaged in the process of involution. They were learning about individualization and in this process were moving further and further away from the One. They were steadily spiraling deeper and deeper into limitation, lack and suffering. Through the lives and examples of these great Teachers, a momentum was established which reversed the trend.

While ultimately everything serves evolution, at that time, distinct tools were presented to humanity to take themselves out of the bog of despair and pain and to reverse the spiral away from God. Now, men and women had tools which even the simplest could use to return to their Source, to return to alignment and unity with the Divine.

At this time there are so many of you that are taking a stand for Truth, that the many lies that have been allowed in your world are being confronted on every level of society. Fear and the lies it generates are no longer acceptable.

At the highest levels of Truth is that which is God's understanding. In Divine's Truth, you are ever held as a perfect child of the Creator. When Truth about any situation is held firmly in your mind, the energies of Love permeate your body and help you to maintain health and wholeness as a reflection of the real Truth of your being.

Some language, some behaviors spiral you away from God; others bring you closer. For example, those words of complaint or criticism, words intended to hurt another or control others for your own selfish purposes, or worse, curses uttered intentionally or carelessly, as though utterly meaningless, are all things of power and are the tools of darkness.

Now that the footsteps of humanity have at last turned toward Home, every cruel word, every distorted thought, every iota of misqualified energy from every lifetime must be cleared and transmuted. As you proceed upon your spiritual path, you will be constantly offered the opportunity to clear these patterns. Each day you will have a bit more to work on. Use the Violet Flame. Each day, you will be expanding your strength and character.

*Each day you will have the opportunity
to work on a bit more karma.*

Right now, the entire planet is working to clear its backlog of debt. You, dear ones, have volunteered to clear some of the accumulated mass of planetary karma so that the planet might continue its ascension process and be raised to the intended level of collective consciousness.

We encourage you to remember that you were extensively trained before you took embodiment (and many are teaching useful techniques in many forms, in case you forgot). Please continue to love and support one another during these transition years. Keep your mind focused on that which is positive and constructive.

The simple rules for your work are as follows:
♦ *Love one another.*
♦ *See the God force in each other and in all life.*
♦ *Give thanks in all things.*
♦ *Ask for help when the job seems too big—and for all the other-sized jobs as well.*

♦ *Focus on where you are going, rather than on what you are trying to avoid or leave behind.*

♦ *Remember Divine Will is your will but with an understanding of the bigger picture. Life is not a torture test.*

♦ *Let go and let God.*

♦ *Ask to have things given to you in a way that you can understand and accept comfortably.*

♦ *Life is filled with joy. Look for it in everything.*

♦ *Whenever you start a sentence with "I Am," you are calling on the name of God—the Creative Force of God. Make sure you want to create what you say next. This is very important write it down and read it over and over until you remember. Every time you say I am sick and tired of..., I am lonely, I am depressed, etc. you are calling on God to give you that!*

If you find that you have filled your mind with habits of speech and behavior that are counterproductive, be aware that there is an amazing opportunity being offered to you now. Many are reporting that it feels as if their minds have gone haywire. They can't remember a whole lot of things. What is happening? You are being given maximum assistance at this time to release all thoughts, thought forms, old programs, and so forth, that no longer serve you. You are being given the opportunity to consciously choose what you want in your mind instead.

It is somewhat like a computer filled with old software. A lot of it doesn't work very well, and some of it has an awful lot of mistakes in it. Well, your brain is in much the same sad state. It would make life a bit too complicated to wipe out everything, so you are dealing with one portion at a time. This is a chance to reprogram your subconscious.

Do you want your cells to install and maintain a rejuvenation process? *Tell them.* Design and install your personal master program for health, well-being, rapid healing, and maximum vitality and beauty. Do you want to only attract relationships of the highest order for joy, play, mutual growth, sacred sexuality, honorable friendship, and so on?

Command your subconscious to do so. You have always had the authority; now you have the understanding that it will be programmed by you, either by conscious choices or by unconscious, and sometimes destructive, thoughts, words and actions.

You have the right to choose your highest and best vision for yourself. Your Soul has been waiting for you for a very long time to take command. It is time now to create a new paradigm for yourself, and as you do so, it joins with the collective shift for all humanity. And you can make sure that your programs are all upgradeable as you find new things you want to add or perfect.

Look at every part of your life. What do you desire? What are you choosing for yourself?

Meaningful work? More joy? More money? Opportunities to serve others in ways that allow everyone to prosper? Love? Challenges? Adventure? Name it and claim it!

You will, of course, notice that some of the old programs haven't been entirely cleared out of the computer banks, yet. This is all right. Write a command to clear them gently and effortlessly. You can add that where it is important that you understand a particular lesson, that it come to you with maximum ease and joy.

What are these commands supposed to look like?

They are simple. The subconscious is not looking for a Master's thesis. Second and third grade language is just fine. The simpler the better. The subconscious particularly likes simple rhymes if you want to try that. It is why advertising jingles work so well.

Exercise 12-1 The Power of the Word

For example, to start, say aloud:
- *I Am commanding...*
- *I command...*
- *With the full authority of my Mighty I Am Presence, I command...*

For Health and Healing add:

I now replace these thoughts with Divine Love and my own, perfect Divine Blueprint for self-maintaining health and wholeness.

For Relationships add
- *the attraction of my Divine right partner to share a healthy, holy, joyful life. (Be as specific as you can about what you desire.)*
- *the strengthening of the bonds of love and trust with those who are my friends, family and co-workers.*

For the Higher Self add
- *the deepening of my bonds of Love and Joy with my Higher Self.*
- *the ability to hear my guidance easily, clearly and effortlessly, with full understanding of right action and right timing.*
- *comfort and healing, ease and grace, during this and all clearing processes.*
- *the ability to remember that I chose my lessons and to smile and laugh more during the process.*

Basically, ask what isn't working the way you want it to in your life. Find the words to clear out the old programs and beliefs. Heal the wounds that might have been created. Nurture the parts of self that need healthy attention. Create a new inner life that satisfies every need for your highest good.

Sound simple? It is. You were programmed as a small child. You made life decisions as an infant and young child. Your parents and friends added their beliefs and programs, society and culture added theirs. Now you can sort through and decide what, if anything, you want to keep. Create your life the way you want it to be now.

Does it sound too good to be true? Try it out. See if you can create your life the way you want it to be. Let the skeptical part of yourself be the judge. Let that part watch the process and evaluate it. Perhaps it can point out why something isn't working. Perhaps there are some factors only an insider can show you. Your inner skeptic is a valuable ally. Perhaps there are other parts of your subconscious that must be addressed, other parts of yourself to get to know: the Inner Child, the body, your inner parents, the inner Rebel, your Inner Healer.

You have a wonderful inner team of counselors and assistants just waiting for a chance to have their lives upgraded; new skills, new talents revealed; new job descriptions given. Find out who you have on your inner "staff." Call a conference. Invite everyone to attend. Maybe some parts are not speaking to one another. Has some part been locked in the dungeon? Get to know yourself. Call on the wisest and most loving part of yourself to help the other parts release the past and start creating the best life you can dream of. Chapter 19 includes a specific exercise for exploring this concept.

What about drug addictions or overweight? Well, why not? These are all things you brought into your life to bring you greater good (as you saw it at the time). Find out what you really wanted then and what you really want now. Why did you choose this instead of that? Can you achieve your goals another way? Choose it now.

These are wondrous days. There are so many amazing

opportunities for change being offered, and we are so pleased that you are finding the ways to avail yourself of them and to assist others in understanding the ease with which such things can now be accomplished.

It doesn't require an explanation that is hard to comprehend. There are psychological systems evolving to redirect speech patterns such as cognitive therapy. There is the idea of conscious language; and many workshops deal with choosing only the very best way to express your desires, your feelings, your choices.

There is a system of hypnotherapy called Neurolinguistic Programming (NLP) and its many techniques. There are the techniques of Alchemical Hypnotherapy and, no doubt, many others being created all the time. There are the decrees, mantras and prayers of sacred scriptures and the Ascended Masters. Most recently, the *Conversations with God* books by Neale Donald Walsch include a number of ideas in this vein.

Mary-Ma McChrist has worked with the Ascended Master teachings since the 1970's and she offers several books of prayers and decrees that are very useful for raising your entire vibrational field as well as your conscious awareness of language and its power to create and transform, to heal and to protect. These include: *Our Daily Bread* and *The Blessed Mother's Blue Rose of the Healing Heart.*

Use language which makes you most comfortable. Many processes are being used with increasing success by all types of people, not just New Agers.

Even the Bible speaks of being "born again" and becoming a new man or woman. There is no limit by belief system. All are enabled to embrace this new understanding of how to be a co-creator or co-commander in this reordering process. It may seem a little strange at first, but after all, who better than you to reset your consciousness. You want to be in charge of your own lives. Here is the perfect opportunity.

"What if I make a mistake and don't like what happens?" you may ask. Well, you have certainly been complaining to beat the band about not liking what you have been creating! Here is an opportunity to do better. It is not fixed in concrete. You may certainly change anything you don't like.

Can't remember what you said? Well, it is perfectly all right to keep a record of what you are creating for yourself and go over it and edit it if you want to. Call it a system upgrade. It is quite a good idea, really. It would be good if you had a record of the programming that is in your mind now. I am sure that you would be surprised to see all the beliefs and ideas that have been ruling your lives.

"Why, I never wanted any of these things," you'd say. Well, here is your chance to say what you do want and what you do mean.

We are going to be offering quite a collection of ideas and suggestions for creating exactly what you do want in your life in these pages. We hope you are pleased with the ideas already presented and are looking forward eagerly to what will come.

Exercises to reprogram the subconscious mind

Setting the field: *Decree: (Say out loud) I call for the Presence of my Higher Self, my Angels,Guides and the beloved Ascended Masters. I give thanks for their help and their assistance today.*

I call for a scintillating tube of White Light to surround and protect me (and, if necessary, another to enfold us as a group). Each tube extends infinitely upward and down into the center of the Earth. I command that this tube be filled with the Violet Flame of Transmutation, so that any energies which come to me or from me may be only of the highest. I give thanks for all the lessons of the past that now allow me to create that which will serve me better as I become a co-creator of Heaven on Earth.

I ask that all that I do today be for my highest good for greater health, greater prosperity, greater love, and greater wisdom and understanding. I communicate now with that portion of myself within the subconscious mind which serves to protect me from all that might harm me. "I thank you for all your service in the past. I ask your assistance today, in union with my Mighty I Am Presence, as I release those programs which no longer serve me and replace them with those I now choose, in order to step forward gently and effortlessly into my next level of expansion in the Light and Love and Power of my own Beloved and Mighty I Am Presence.

Bring to my attention those words and ideas which are best suited to my own individual needs. I further command that all changes created today are suitable for further clarification and upgrading at any time in the future.

Exercise 12-2: Hands *(This exercise may be done with any part of the body.)*

Sit or lie down. Find a very comfortable position. Allow yourself to remember yourself as an infant. Let yourself look at the wonder of your hands. Remember a time when they were almost completely out of control. Over time they became tools of exquisite sensitivity. Imagine yourself holding this infant you and feeling a great love wash through you as look at the child and its tiny hands filled with such potential.

Spend a moment now looking at your grown-up hands. Draw a picture of your hands (Get some paper and pen or pencil and spend about 5 minutes).

Next, create a visual memory of ten things your hands do to bring you pleasure or joy. Make a list. Draw another picture of your hand.

When you have finished, notice if there are any differences in the way you looked at your hands. Did spending some time appreciating your hands help you to see them differently? (The first time I, Mikaelah, did this exercise, I raced through the first drawing; the second one was made with greater care and attention and much greater appreciation.) Your hands are tools of wondrous power to heal, to bless, to give and receive. Remember to take the time to honor their gift to you. What would happen if we took the time to think of ten things we appreciate about one another? Would we see each other differently?

Decree: *I call forth my Mighty I Am Presence to release from every cell and atom of my being, every record, memory, pattern and trace of any ways in which my hands have ever been used to harm anyone or anything, or any ways in which I have been harmed by another's hands in this or any lifetime. May these energies be released now and forever into the Violet Flame of Transmutation and Forgiveness.*

Through the Light and the Might of my own Beloved I Am Presence, I command that my hands are instruments for the expression of Divine Perfection and my portion of the Divine Plan for my life and the world. I now call for a Golden Sun to shine over the crown of my head. I draw this brilliant white and gold light down through my crown chakra into my third eye, reframing and reprogramming the conscious and subconscious mind and all the nerve pathways of my physical brain for the dedication of my hands to bless, to heal, and to serve the Light and the Love of God/Goddess/All that Is. I draw this white and gold light down into my heart and out through my arms and hands.

Decree: *I ask for a blessing to pour forth from the Infinite Source of all Love through my hands to bless and heal the Earth, particularly those records having to do with the misqualification of energy through the use of the hands. I call for the Angels and the Archangels of the Violet Flame to forever transmute these energies from past, present, and future through all dimensional realities and all lifetimes. I visualize a Violet Flame encompassing the Earth and ask that it completely consume all such misqualified energies. I replace such records from the collective consciousness with the ideas of the hands as sacred instruments of the Divine. (You might wish to write down your vision and/or share it if you are working in a group.)*

Exercise 12-3: Healing and Unconditional Love
(Best done with a partner—but, if working alone, visualize a partner.)

Create a grounding cord with your imagination from the base of your spine and allow it to fall deep into the center of the Earth. Begin attuning within yourself through your breath. Breathe in and out, slowly and gently moving into a place of peacefulness and deeper and deeper receptivity. Allow your focus to expand outward from your own body to include the Earth.

Call for the creation of a tube of white light of protection and purity to surround you easily and gently, extending infinitely upward and down into the center of the Earth. You may ask that this column of light be surrounded with the Violet Flame for transmutation of any negativity that may be in the energy that you are receiving throughout the day.

Continue to follow the breath, drawing on the energies of unconditional Love that fill and emanate from the Earth. Notice the color, the sound, the feeling of these Love energies.

Draw them up through your feet with each breath, allowing the Light to flow up your legs, past your hips, and allowing the Light to collect in your pelvic area.

Now, move your attention to the Love energies of the universe, of the cosmos. Use the breath to draw them down from the heavenly dimensions through the crown of your head, down the spinal column, all the way down to the pelvic area to combine with the Earth energies. Allow these energies to mix and blend here, and then move upward, gently swirling and cleansing through each chakra. Gently breathe in and out through each chakra:

first, base of the spine—survival and procreation;
second, below the umbilicus—emotions, sexuality;
third, solar plexus—power center;
fourth, heart area—love, relationships;
fifth, throat area—communication;
sixth, brow—third eye, clairvoyance, the mind;
seventh, crown of head—spiritual connection.

Turning your attention to the heart, allow these combined Earth and Cosmic energies of unconditional Love to flow up through the shoulders, through your arms and out your hands. Ask permission to share this Love with your partner. Take turns. Feel, hear or see (use all your senses) a place of pain or discomfort in your partner where they are willing to receive Love and Healing energy.

Place your hands on or over this part and allow the green and gold Love Light (other colors are OK, too) of Earth and Cosmic Love from Father/Mother God/All That Is to flow through you, through your heart and your hands to your partner, so that they may receive healing and blessing for their highest good. (Don't try to tell the universe what that is supposed to look like, please.) You might think words of love, comfort, healing or blessing for them as the Light flows through you. Allow it to move until it reaches a point of completion. Then gently call back all of your own energy, leaving them with the Love that has flowed through you. Release and return to them any energy that is theirs that you might have taken on. All energies are purified and transmuted as they pass through the Violet Flame in your tubes of light. Take a few deep breaths and return your full attention to the present moment.

Exercise 12-4: Healing eyes, ears, nose, mouth, organs of touch; claiming Life and rejuvenation; cessation of the death hormone.

Imagine your infant self again. You were pure, innocent, open. Let all the things your eyes have seen which led to discomfort or fear pass across your memory. Once again calling on the Violet Flame, let these memories pass through the flame of transmutation and forgiveness as you retain the lessons with the highest possible understanding and wisdom for your future actions and choices.

Your eyes have seen enough of fear and pain, death, horror and destruction. Let it all go into the flame. Let it unroll like a reel of film to be forever transmuted in the flames. Let the flames grow and dance until they become a pillar, a wall, a world of Violet Flame, consuming and transmuting the ugliness, the evil, the sightless and the lightless. The eyes are the windows of the soul. Let the soul memories of all less than beauty and perfection be released into the flame. Let the flame transmute to the roots of your cellular records, your RNA and DNA, the very atomic spin and orbit. Let all be cleansed.

Decree: *I call for the full and complete clearing of the physical body, the emotional body, the mental body, and the etheric body. I call for the complete alignment of all four lower bodies with the Divine Blueprint for perfection held at the*

level of Christ Consciousness (5th layer of the aura).
The child reflects the heavenly realms in its innocent state. Reclaim your heavenly home within you as you begin to see with new eyes and perceive with renewed senses. Allow more of heaven to shine through your eyes into the world.

Bring in Light through your eyes and in through the crown of your head and cleanse the pituitary and pineal glands. It is time now to reset the program for death to one for Life and rejuvenation.

Decree: *In the name of my Mighty I Am Presence, I command that I am forever released from the energies of involution and death. I call for the activation and replenishment of the hormone which renews and rejuvenates every cell in my body. I am now redirecting my attention and all the energies of Life toward ever-expanding health, beauty, love, prosperity, joy and wisdom for my highest good and that of all Life.*

Cleansing the Ears: *As with the eyes, reflect briefly on the volumes of criticism, cruelty, teasing, slurs, curses, and fearful sounds of anger, hatred, rejection, disharmony and destruction—every discordant sound and misqualified energy coming to our ears, whether inner or outer. We allow all to pass through the Violet Consuming Flame, from the remotest past up to the present, from every dimensional reality; and we release it purified back into the infinite. We ask that all that has passed our ears and our hearing that is of Love, Truth, Beauty, Joy, Clarity, and Wisdom be expanded and that we now draw to us those circumstances that will continue to add to our record and memory that which brings us greater attainment through our hearing, both inner and outer, with perfection and the greatness of Life. We remind ourselves to ever focus on that which is harmonious and uplifting, in both our own speech and that to which we listen.*

Continue this process with the senses of smell, taste, and touch. Focus on specific memories and patterns of the past that are troubling you at this time. Clear with the Violet Flame and replace with the commands you now choose for your Highest Good.

For further cleansing and integration, you may use the medium of art to represent the energies of change, from what was to what will be. You may wish to draw with colored pens, crayons or paints. Some prefer a free form abstract approach, others something representational. Follow your intuition here. This will work on those levels beyond language as you set your intention. You may also choose to use dance and movement to integrate these changes in all the four lower bodies.

Merely stand up and allow yourself to move freely as you feel the shifting that is now occurring within you. Your body knows what it needs to do to move energies. You may wish to use music or not.

In conclusion, give thanks to God/Goddess /All That Is for all the Love, Healing and Blessings that come to you daily.

Chapter Thirteen

The Role of the Elementals

Lord Sunanda Speaks

Beloved Ones, I Am Sunanda. We are here with you because there is that of which we would speak today. It is of the role of the Elementals, beloved ones—those beings who are at the initial stage of the Elohim lineage. They are the creators of form at the basic levels.

We speak of and for the elementals because it is vastly important that you know and understand who they are and what they do. In this vast wave of becoming that is sweeping the Earth, it is necessary to examine who you are and who you have been in order to move successfully toward who and what you will be.

In the illusions of separation, you experienced yourselves as separate from God, separate from the Angels, separate from one another, separate from the life force directing and ensouling the mineral, plant and animal kingdoms. The end result was to be separated from yourself.

In the consciousness of Unity, you will know that all is a giant package of interconnected parts. Your thoughts and feelings directly affect those around you, and that includes the life and consciousness of the elementals—the spirits of the rocks, plants, animals, air, earth, fire, water, and ether—indeed, the very machinery that you have manufactured as your servants.

What does this mean?

It means, no longer can you ascribe to "accidents" or "bad luck" the negative circumstances of your life. You have created these with your choices. And ignorance and inaction are equally choices, as are knowledge and action.

We do not wish to seem cruel, judgmental or harsh here. But we do wish you to claim your power, to claim your authority, to claim your full mastery over your lives.

The fear that you have lived with for far too long is that you would make a "mistake" (God forbid) and create some kind of huge disaster, if you had any kind of real power.

Memories of the destruction of Maldek (*once a sister planet to Earth, its fragments are now an asteroid belt*), the destruction and fall of Atlantis due to certain misuse of power and crystal technology, of Adam and Eve and their disobedience, even of the rebellion and subsequent fall of certain of the Angels—all fill your souls with horror. Look what could happen if I misused power or made a bad choice. *I don't want it!*

Well, beloveds, you have power whether you want it or not. Closing your eyes and your minds to the truth of it does not make it go away.

Imagine what would happen if every infant said, "No, I will not stand up or take a step. I might fall or look foolish." Fortunately, no such thought enters their minds. In innocence and trust they follow their inner drives for mastery of their bodies and their worlds.

Somewhere along the way of growth and acculturation that innocence and trust get lost. But, even so, most of you are still able to walk and talk.

Claiming your mastery includes being able to see that possible disasters, obvious or unforeseen, might accompany your choices and acting anyway. It means acting from your highest point of understanding and integrity, not knowing all the possible outcomes, but choosing to live your life and not trying constantly to second guess it.

There are *always* going to be forces at work of which you have no understanding. You will not know if or when the Western half of the United States will sink under the ocean. You will not always know whether there is contamination in your food or water supply, or when you will have a flat tire, or for that matter, why.

Still, you are challenged to act in the world. You are challenged to see where your assistance can make a difference and to offer it. Maybe you will be rejected. Maybe it will take centuries before your gifts will be acknowledged, but now is the time to give of yourself—to share of your uniqueness.

It is the desire of the elementals
to work with you in the co-creation
of this New Heaven and New Earth

And we speak to you of the elementals at this time, because it is their desire to work with you in the co-creation of this New Heaven and New Earth.

Let us start with your bodies, beloved ones. Your bodies are composed of many complex parts interacting and integrated into a unified whole.

There was a very funny story told by Jane Roberts in one of her *Seth* books of what happened when her oversoul gave her hand "free will" for a day. She would reach for something, intending to pick it up, and knock it down or scratch her nose instead. Here was a small, but significant, understanding. Think about it. The whole must work together to accomplish anything. She learned much from this exercise; perhaps we can learn much from her story.

So let us start by introducing you to the elementals of your body. There is a consciousness that lives and works within each particle and atom of your being, as well as a consciousness of what you call your stomach, your skin, your heart, your blood, your hair, your feet, etc. And over all there is one who is the chief—one who manages everything. You have noticed that when you are asleep or meditating or soul traveling, your body keeps breathing, digesting, blood circulates, and so on, have you not? Who or what do you think drives your car when your mind is elsewhere?

We ask you to begin to listen to the wisdom of your body. Let us start with a simple exercise of talking with your feet.

Exercise 13-1 Dialogue with your feet

(You might wish to have a notebook handy to write your thoughts as you complete the following exercise. You might also wish to read this once over and then close your eyes and follow the instructions. You might also choose to read it aloud and record it and replay it so you can listen with your eyes closed and your attention focused.)

Let yourself sit quietly for a moment and imagine that it is possible to talk with parts of yourself, even your feet. Imagine that you have an inner room where you can go to have this conversation with your feet. Imagine what it would look like and how it feels to sit there. Look, listen, smell and feel what this place is like.

Observe your surroundings and know that it is very possible to do this. Allow yourself to include whatever you like to make this room comfortable and personal. Perhaps some cozy chairs, pictures on the wall, or a fireplace would feel good to you. And let yourself pretend, if you need to call it that, that you can also create a dialogue that has meaning for you.

Sit quietly, close your eyes and imagine that you are following your breath. Quietly and gently start by noticing the breath as it goes in and out several times. Next, begin to imagine the breath flowing all the way down through your body to your feet. It continues to flow, in and out, down the length of your body.

Allow your attention to flow with the breath down into your feet. Notice any sensations you may feel. Do you see any colors or hear any sounds? Just breathe and notice for a minute. Then send love and appreciation to your feet. Start by saying, "thank you." Perhaps you've been ignoring your feet or taking them for granted. Remember now all the services that they provide for you. (If you are among the minority who have feet that don't function or are missing, imagine what your feet would have liked to do for you. And thank them for their sacrifice for the whole.) If your feet are whole, perhaps you can take a moment to pray for those whose feet are not.

And then return your attention to your feet. Do your feet like to be touched or massaged? Most of you can do this for yourself. Take a moment now and touch your feet consciously and lovingly. Or imagine that your etheric hands can reach down and lovingly touch your feet or your etheric feet.

Ask your feet to communicate to you some message that is important to them and to you. Allow your feet to offer their suggestions, thoughts, or ideas. Feet are pretty much down-to-earth. Don't expect too much abstract philosophy. But you might hear some very practical advice. Usually, we are too busy to even think about communicating like this, but it is valuable to slow down and listen to our body.

If you find it easier to tell yourself that you are "imagining" what they might say, go ahead. Ask that your conscious (and often critical) mind step aside and just observe what is happening without judgment or limitation.

Please stop here and listen to your own message before going on to read what I heard. I do not wish for my ideas to create limits for you. Use your paper and pen to write down the thoughts or even to record the dialogue as it comes to you.

(Author's note: The first time I did this exercise I heard, "Buy more comfortable shoes." The ones I wore hurt my feet. Today I heard, "Use some lotion with vitamins A and E in it on us. And get two hours of sun every day. Take my shoes off and walk in the grass, touch the Earth. Learn to listen with your feet. We will tell you when a direction is good for you or not. We are in touch with the elementals of the Earth. Too much washing is not good for us. Put oil or cream on before and after a bath. (This has done wonders for my dry and cracked heels.)

"Walk with us as partners. Let us bring you to some new situations. Let us move more freely as we dance. Let the toes wiggle. Give us more freedom. We will take you where you want to go."

And now, let your attention move to your hands. Look at them. Think of ten things they do for you. Look at all the ways that hands are used to interact with others: shaking hands, signaling, sharing, cooking, patting, games, writing, touching ourselves, touching each other.

Say, "Thank you." Hold one hand with the other. Wonderful servants—do we honor them or abuse them? Repeat the previous exercise, this time with your hands. Before reading what I received, explore and record your own experiences.

Mikaelah's hand speaks to her: "Mother, you are too hard on yourself. You are always holding yourself back from what you really **want** *to do. You are forcing yourself to do what you don't want to do. Even that computer game is to keep you from doing what you really want to do.*

"How about trusting yourself? Yes, there is work to do and we love to do it.

"Let yourself love what you are doing. Put all of your attention into what you are doing. You are spending an awful lot of your time with just an eensy teensy part of you paying attention. Be fully present. Stop running away from your life.

"If you are going to do something, do it!

"Where is the rest of you anyway? I'll help you do whatever you want, but be here (aware) while you do it."

There is a new idea emerging about the role of the elementals. They are desirous of becoming co-creators with you on your path.

As you dialogue with various parts of your body - the physical elemental, you might ask, "How can you help me on my path? How can you help me to be more joyful, more fulfilled, more able to bring forth the sacred in every moment?" The answers might surprise you. Your feet might give you some hints on how to work with them when deciding which choice to make or which direction to go. Your stomach or digestive system might suggest when to eat, what to eat or drink, and how often for the maximum perfection of your physical vehicle and your increasing ability to hold and emanate light. Your eyes may have a suggestion that will be related to their role. Each part of you is becoming more spiritualized, more unified, more inspired.

As you take the time to communicate and to really listen and honor what you hear, the relationship will continue to expand and to grow in directions you have never anticipated. This is experimental. Humanity has not used this approach before. Many holy people have ignored or punished the body in the past. Now we are to fully spiritualize matter and its role is becoming yet another of the unfolding miracles that surround us daily.

Exercise 13-2: Establishing clear personal yes-no signals.

Sit quietly and focus on the breath and the heart for three minutes or so. Ask that you be clear and balanced.

Option One: In this exercise your body acts as a pendulum. You stand with both hands over your heart and ask a yes or no question. If the answer is yes, you sway forward. If no, you sway backward. (Some individuals find that their body gives slightly different signals here, check what is true for you.) Sometimes there is no change and the answer is uncertain or the question unclear. There can be a great deal of subtle variation in this method. For example, if you stand still for a while and then slowly sway forward, this may mean, "yes, but later." Experience will teach you here.

Option Two: Open your eyes and say: "I call for my own Christ Self, my Buddha Self (nature), my I Am Presence to give me a personal signal that is clear, simple and easily recognized when I ask for your confirmation of my questions or requests.

Now say, "Please show me now the signal for yes." The signal may be physical—body twitching, right hand or finger moving, head nods, tingling sensation through your body (truth rush), or whatever you choose. If it is too subtle, ask for something else until you are satisfied.

You might ask for it to repeat twice if you need to be certain. Etheric signs might be music, color, or feelings. You might hear "yes." Close your eyes, return your focus to the breath, and receive your signal.

Repeat the exercise for your "no" signal.

(For those for whom this doesn't work well, use something that does.)

Use these signals to check for completeness or clarity as in: "Am I clear?" "Is this complete?" "Do I need further help?" "Is this all I can do now?"

Regular use of the signals helps you to establish confidence and trust based on experience, not theory.

I particularly encourage you to use the technique many times a day on simple choices with no emotional content. Such as: should I buy carrots or broccoli for dinner tonight? Are these apples better or this type over here? Which movie would be better tonight? In this way you develop confidence without having to trust your life savings to a decision based on something you've no experience with.

If you have difficulties with this chapter or any of the exercises, there are Lightworkers around the world who have a variety of different kinds of training who can give you the assistance you need. Ask your Angels to bring the right help to your attention and to give you the trust and the willingness to receive their help.

If you have resistance to this material, be open to the possibility of the idea that it is because it is something that you have been unwilling to look at or accept.

Also remember that, as your journey progresses, there may be new things that come up at different levels of consciousness that were inaccessible to you before. You may wish to repeat these exercises then or at any time.

Chapter Fourteen

Signs and Wonders

Jesus Speaks:

Beloved Ones, it is necessary at this time to pay attention to the signs and wonders of your life. There are many signs directing you. Go this way, do this, don't do that. Here is where your heart lies.

You will find that frequently you are so tangled up in listening to what others like or don't like, want or don't want, that you are having a bit of trouble finding out what you really want.

So, pay attention to the details of your life. Part of you has drawn this to you so that you could pay attention to something that you have been ignoring.

> *Pay attention to your inner promptings.*
> *Here is where your heart lies.*

Dear ones, your lives could be much easier *if you would only pay attention to your inner promptings.*

One of the things we wish to do here is to share the simple tools you need for your everyday activities. As the light continues to grow on Earth, more and more that has been buried in the subconscious must come up to be dealt with. It just won't stay hidden and decently buried.

No matter what your level of evolution, there will be "stuff" to deal with. If not yours, then there is lots of family karma, as well as racial, religious, gender, age, national and planetary karmic issues for which you will be responsible.

Those in Great Britain must deal with the issues of a monarchy—what purpose does it serve today and what are the values received by the population? The "Royals" have to deal with whether their soul purposes can be filled in roles that are over 1000 years old. The British are also responsible for the effects that they have had in their centuries of global rule.

Americans must deal with the racial issues of our melting pot society, individual freedom and responsibility.

The Japanese are dealing with personal versus group identity and social norms.

The Chinese are dealing with centuries of poverty, abuse, animistic magical thinking, combined with the ancient wisdom of the Taoist Masters and an overlay of 60 years of chaos and anti-God propaganda mixed with social, cultural and economic reform.

Russians are dealing with the issues of "Com"unity by force, centuries of repression and abuse coupled with a national soul of great artistry and passion.

Each country has its essential character and nature. Each has its gifts—both in terms of natural resources and the physical and mental labor of the people as well as its essential nature—its unique part of the whole dynamic of the planet.

There is a joke about the difference between heaven and hell. In heaven, the French do the cooking, the British run the government, the Swiss run the police, the Germans do the engineering and the Italians do the loving.

In hell, the French do the engineering, the British do the cooking, the Swiss do the loving, the Germans run the police, and the Italians run the government.

Now each individual in a country has his or her own unique gifts and talents—but if this joke made you laugh, then you see that there are strengths and weaknesses we carry as nations as well as individuals.

Can we as individuals honor our gifts and strengths and find our own perfect niche? Can we honor the individual strengths of various nations? Then we can become a unified and productive whole which is the expression of the Divine Plan. If we can do this for ourselves and our children, it will extend to our nations. Then we will be living in the harmony and joy of heaven instead of the disfunctionality and pain of hell.

A Look at the Earth

Beloved ones, let us look for a moment at the atmosphere surrounding the Earth.

There are spaceships surrounding the Earth whose primary mission is to look at the energetic patterns of collective humanity, the emotional and mental bands around the Earth, to identify trouble spots. They then direct those on Earth who are co-workers in form to focus their attention and their healing skills toward ensuring the greatest health and wholeness.

First, we will look at what is happening, selecting a few key global points. Then we will direct your attention to the work of the planetary healers and suggest ways that all might join in these efforts. And for those already so engaged, how you might increase the effectiveness of your time, energy and attention.

Allow yourself to imagine that you are standing before a viewscreen in the command center of a large spaceship. Before you is the Earth. The screen is over twelve feet high and thirty feet wide. To the right of the screen are a number of dials that enable you to gain a closer look at various situations or to show the overlays of the collective emotional energy and the collective mental energy. Highly skilled professionals are familiar with the color patterns and what they represent in terms of overall global energy—from health, harmony and peace to rage, destruction and disease.

Another room is filled with specialized equipment that is

monitoring the sound patterns on Earth—from traffic noises, individuals singing in the shower or whistling at work, to rock concerts, atomic explosions, birds singing, and troops marching. Individually and collectively, the sounds are a significant measure of what is happening and going to happen on Earth. Sound is part of the creative force of God. "In the beginning was the Word ..." (John:1-1). And these collective harmonic patterns will determine the immediate patterns of change on Earth (that is, within two to three weeks).

Just as troops marching in unison can create sound waves that will destroy a bridge, so various sounds foster growth or destruction within plants, animals, individuals, families, groups, organizations, nations and various physical earth structures. (A Biblical example is when Joshua marched his troops around Jericho, blew his trumpet and the walls fell down.)

In the first room, the technicians are sharing a few key sectors with us to give an understanding of the patterns with which they are working.

The first sector under exploration is **Bosnia**. It is as though waves of denser light patterns wash over this area from several directions. Expanding the focus to include most of Eastern/Central Europe, you can see that Bosnia is a point of confluence for small energy patterns that run like the tributaries of a river toward the central point. These end up magnified and focalized in one area (Bosnia) much like the "identified patient" in a family with serious relational problems. In truth, it is the release point for the collective rage, frustration and confusion which surfaced following the fall of Communism. Communism kept these emotional energies repressed through fear. When the increasing light frequencies on Earth forced the dissolution of fear-based structures, then these accumulated feelings had to emerge.

The apparitions of Mother Mary in Medjudgorje were

part of the response of the heavenly realms to the cries for help from Earth. The devotional prayers and focus on her works and miracles that were generated, helped to create a focus of love and healing to counterbalance the massive release of pain and suffering.

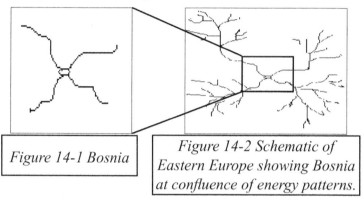

| *Figure 14-1 Bosnia* | *Figure 14-2 Schematic of Eastern Europe showing Bosnia at confluence of energy patterns.* |

Your prayers for the people who suffered under communism and are still suffering from its aftermath are making a difference. And there continues to be a need for a significant increase in meditation, decrees and prayers for these peoples. This is also true for the pain and suffering simmering in the Middle East.

The Influence of Sound Patterns

To give an idea of the sound patterns monitored here, the sound technicians are showing us what a healthy countryside shows compared to the current sound patterns.

In healthy situations, birds and insects, water and wind work together creating a flowing symphony in which human patterns (which tend to be somewhat chaotic—hence destructive) are absorbed.

Trees play a significant role here as they also break up the patterns of the sound of the wind with their leaves, this yields very high frequency modulations in harmonic resonance with the lower base notes of the vibrational pattern or "heart beat" of the Earth.

Large mountain ranges hold these base note patterns and help the surrounding countryside (and the people, animals and plants that live there) to stay in harmony.

Atomic explosions and testing, huge war efforts with guns, tanks, marching soldiers, explosions, and so on create massive patterns of disharmony which lead to distortions in the healthy patterns of the Earth itself, that is, in the energetic fields (or aura) that surround the planet.

As a living organism, the Earth's self-healing powers allow her to repair herself, given enough peace in which to do it. The attacks on all sides are significantly interfering with her powers of recuperation.

We wish to pinpoint three other sites that may be less obvious to you and the impacts that are affecting the Earth. We will not go into detail on the destruction of the rain forests and the damage to the oceans, which are well documented already, but as you can see from what we are saying, they too play a significant role in the Earth changes we are now experiencing.

The Influences of Black Magic

The next site we wish to point out to you is *India*. Here there is a reversal in the damaging effect of centuries of black magic and on a lesser, but no less destructive level—human greed.

India had been a center for great spiritual wisdom and vast wealth shared by the people in the distant past. During the Age of Kali, these civilizations of culture, beauty, science and deep spiritual attunement were overthrown by lesser cultures on a rampage.

In the attempts to identify ways to stop this overwhelming destruction, certain yogic adepts began to misuse their powers. Over time, this misuse of power became focalized in a secret organization which actually completely destroyed the true strength and wealth of India, channeling the vast resources of the people and the land into the hands of a few key individuals who used that to further expand their power and influence. There are remnants of these powerful organizations still operating today. Their major influence was in the 13-14th and the 18-19th centuries, because certain individuals rose to power at those times who could take advantage of world patterns. The British residency in India actually created a situation (mostly unconsciously) which reversed this pattern and allowed the sleeping giant to awaken. Gandhi appeared at a pivotal point to focus the hearts and minds of his people on freedom and reclaiming their power—as represented by the leaving of the British Raj—and reclaiming their heritage symbolically by weaving their own cloth again and keeping their money and power at home.

Coincidentally, the arrival of the British created the opportunity for the transfer of the dark adept brotherhood to first a British and then an Andalusian base in the mid-19th century. From this base were directed World Wars I and II, which were further attempts to channel world resources into war machinery, materiel, etc., and into the pockets of certain industrialists and key financial houses.

We wish to point out to you that the so-called Illuminati are for the most part the operational/financial arm of this dark brotherhood—few of whom have ever been identified, even by the top figures of the Illuminati. They, unfortunately, choose to turn a blind eye to who is really controlling things, as long as they have the illusion of power.

This dark brotherhood has been *vastly* crippled over the last 30 years due to the rise in power—the awakening—of the Lightworkers across the planet, and also due to the cumulative prayers of vast numbers of humanity. Literally thousands of Lightworkers are working independently, or in small groups of two to three, to counter centuries of misuse of power, all under Divine Guidance.

Because this is a Divine Expression, there has been a steady dismantling of the linkages of these hidden power sources to those who attempt world domination through their manipulation, especially those dark adepts attempting to tap the forces of Cosmic Evil through extraterrestrial linkages and a variety of other sources of distorted power.

Hence, the dismantling of the Berlin Wall, the fall of European communism, the release of Russia due largely to the brilliant efforts of Mikhail Gorbachev who was released from domination by a dark force energy (the same that controlled first Hitler and then Stalin). At a key moment in world history, Gorbachev was overshadowed by Archangel Michael. Gorbachev then single-handedly turned his country around before those in power knew what was really happening.

But back to the point about India. Numerous spiritual teachers and gurus are touching the lives of thousands—millions. We wish to particularly focus your attention here on the simple life and work of Mother Teresa and her band of devoted servers. By working according to Divine Wisdom, with the poorest of the poor (judged as of no worth to anyone by those in power, if not most of us), she single-mindedly, one step at a time, in the tradition of humility and service of St. Francis of Assisi and her namesake St. Therése of Lisieux, built a worldwide organization—one step—one drop at a time—until the ocean of compassion that now flows around the world is the most significant step for change for the good ever seen on this Earth.

(This section was written shortly after her death and we hereby pay tribute to the greatness of her soul and her willingness to serve which now places her in the top ranks of the Saints of heaven.)

The poverty in India is a direct influence of the draining

Chapter Fifteen

Planetary Chakras

Lord Sunanda speaks:

Beloved, we are with you today—always. I Am your Sun. We would, indeed, speak today of Hawaii and the elementals there. There is such joy at the ever-expanding blessing that is touching Hawaii at this time. The ancient Lemurian energies there are of a time that was very high, very etheric.

These ancient and very beautiful patterns were experiencing much distortion in the face of Western culture and technology and the focus on making money in a fashion that was in conflict with the rhythms of the land.

Over the last few years, there has come to be a balancing of these two patterns, so there is somewhat more harmony now. That which is not in harmony with the land will gradually be removed or redirected.

Hawaii is the planetary center for Harmony and Beauty (Ninth Ray energy). The combination of oceanic energies, especially as enhanced by the whales and their song frequencies, allows for Air, Earth, Fire and Water to interact very powerfully and synergistically. It is a very creative energy here. The mountains, volcanoes, the wind, rain and ocean.

Primal energies are able to merge here. The people

who live here must be able to work with these forces within themselves.

That which is out of alignment will be bounced and blown ever to the outer edge to be removed.

It is not truly a place of rest and relaxation, as so many have thought. Rather it is a place of great expansion and growth, of rejuvenation.

On the surface it may seem peaceful and restful. In the depths it is filled with primal power, birthing the new. From Hawaii comes the primal pattern of the Earth. The whales pick up the harmonics and whale song relays it around the globe.

The new frequencies of Earth were birthed through Hawaii. It is a Sirian energy, the frequency of blue.

The mountains are the least stable part of this combination of air, earth, fire and water. Barely can the land balance the massive frequencies which come together here.

This will soon result in the calling forth once again of the large land masses of Lemurian lineage, now far beneath the oceans. These mountains must rise to hold the patterns of life now emerging on Earth.

Of necessity, the rising of such massive amounts of land will cause a falling away elsewhere to balance it. By 2017, these great land shifts will become very obvious.

There will be both some very rapid changes and those which are very slow. There will be evolutionary changes of the kind which are more familiar to you. You may anticipate massive land adjustments over the next 2,000 years. The next 200 years will be the most dramatic.

We would speak to you next of Uhuru in Australia (Ayer's Rock area). This is very sacred land and has been held as uninhabitable except by the dedicated few.

The Aborigines have held this power point of the Earth as a sacred trust for thousands of years. Their attunement to the Earth, their mobility, the walkabout, has often been the primary thing holding the Earth together through these times of darkness. They, and they alone, walked the patterns of the Universe and linked them with the Earth's grid, holding the safety, indeed the very existence of the Earth, through their daily acts of unity with the invisible worlds as they integrated trans-universal energies.

We would speak of Mt. Kailash in Tibet next. The frequencies of Light held here in the highest mountains of the world are dispersed now, held in the etheric vehicles of certain Tibetan monks, and anchored and relayed at various minor chakra points on their journeys.

The centers of power there have been deactivated. Once it was a seed point for the highest mental energies entering Earth and responsible for the attunements of the higher mental plane around the planet.

Now, Lightworkers around the Earth are collectively rebuilding the mental planes through sacred song, prayer, decrees and affirmations. It is not yet time for the rededication of the new power point. Those who are active on the Yellow Gold Ray of Illumination and Enlightenment—of the Buddha—will be key to the final designation. It will not be in place again until after the major land mass shifts have occurred. It is now being held temporarily at a secret location that is not for public release.

Another major point, Mt. Fuji, has also been deactivated in anticipation of the shifts in land masses. Mt. Denali in Alaska now holds the activation for this planetary field, the Root chakra. Mt. Denali is the true name for what is now called Mt. McKinley. This newer name should be changed as it cannot hold the vibration that Denali represents.

As the land mass shifts and the poles rotate, Mt. Denali will be in a much more fertile and temperate climate zone. There will most certainly be a melting of the polar ice caps. Yes, this will happen soon—within ten years *(received September, 1997 and referring to the polar shift, meaning before 2007).*

Update as of October, 2002: There will be no dramatic polar shift of the kind that we spoke of earlier. This circumstance has been drastically altered by several significant choices by certain groups of humanity. For the most part the changes we have described in this section will continue exactly as we have indicated. However, this particular change—that of a Polar Shift—will happen in a more gradual and less-destsructive way. Rather than cataclysmic, the entire planet will be shifting into the fifth dimension, and the changes that are resultant from that shift will be of a far more gentle and harmonious form than some prophecieshave suggested.

The most significant of these world altering choices is described in a new chapter we placed at the very end of this book.

We have left the preceding paragraphs in place so that those who wish to compare the differences between the first and second edition of this book might do so most readily.)

Native American traditional ways will be the key to this transition. Drumming and dancing will set the field for the structuring of the new patterns here in North America. Each tribe, in its own ways of ritual, music and dance, will hold a unique piece of the mosaic that is being formed. This will extend as far south as Central America and will happen in a natural way according to the traditional and cultural patterns of various tribes.

Certain beats within contemporary rock music (we will not say which ones) have served to break up the old patterns both in individuals and for the Earth. Look at the changes that you can see since the 1950's. These are a direct consequence of the musical patterns introduced to the world and known as Rock and Roll. The new emerging patterns, however, will require a slower, deeper rhythm—a full attunement to Mother Earth as she takes on her new garment of Light. The purer the alignment with the ancient ways, the clearer will be the emergence here.

Here will be the weaving of the Light, through sacred song and sacred dance, into the etheric framework. This will be the building of the more detailed patterns on the basic frameworks that are now in place. As the patterns are expanded, there will then be the possibility of the more highly refined attunements, and the patterns will be adjusted accordingly in incremental steps. Thus, this will be not an overnight accomplishment, but will take place over many years. Indeed, it will be an ongoing process of constant improvement and incremental change.

Mt. Denali holds the heart beat for this music and the alignment of the Earth with the Light. From here will come the attunements necessary for finding right livelihood—of the integration of individual and earth patterns for the good of the whole.

In South America, Machu Picchu holds the Emerald Ray and the reemerging of the Sacred Healing Temples. A key crystal is buried here. The focus on Machu Picchu as a tourist site must give way to its true nature as a key activation point and intergalactic gateway. Indeed, tourism will grow and expand greatly as it is returned to "active duty." It will become a fully active site in the not too distant future.

Lake Titicaca in Peru will see the reopening of the Temple of the Sun (one of several sites to be so designated around the Earth). Pleiadean energies are strong there. The new religion will recognize this as a sacred site. This will emerge when the energies of synthesis allow the walls of separation to fall away between the existing religions, Again, local politics may interfere temporarily with its true expression.

Palenque in Mexico—once the location of an ancient and sacred religion and a major power center— it is still too contaminated to serve and will be fully deactivated.

Update as of April, 2000: We wish to commend the work of the many who have traveled to Palenque and other meso-American sites for the purposes of planetary healing. That which has been harmed is at the level of core energetics of the former Earth matrix. It cannot be corrected without massive loss of life in the region. This is not considered to be either necessary or useful.

Rather, it will be allowed to remain as a reminder of that which can happen when limited consciousness attempts to rearrange the world and its forces to suit a more limited purpose. It will not be an impediment in any way to the activation and fulfillment of the Divine Plan as it is now being expressed on Earth.

This is neither the time nor the place to go into more detail on this matter. If there is sufficient interest in this and other planetary healing matters, we suggest that those so interested call an international conclave to explore and address such interests.

Indeed it would be of some merit to begin gathering as much information as can be detailed in terms of an historical documentation of this time from those involved. It is no longer necessary to maintain the veils of secrecy about your identities or your work that have been required in the past. If any feel that they need to remain veiled, please continue to do so. We would say, however, that this work is fifth dimensional and higher, and no matter what the outer political climate, it cannot be understood by those in lower dimensional consciousness and is not taken seriously.

The new site replacing Palenque will be in the emerging Atlantean land mass. It will be several hundred years before it can be considered usable. In the meantime, the site of the Statue of Jesus overlooking Rio de Janeiro in Brazil will serve as a temporary focal point for linking certain energy flows from a number of galactic transmitters.

Stonehenge in Great Britain is still in the process of being brought back to its full activation potential. Again the tourist focus will have to give way to its rededication to service as a planetary "battery." Those who are being trained now on inner levels are being moved into position for their work here that is both sacred and scientific. Certain key transmissions will be focalized through this ring of stones. Part of the Song of the Universe will be relayed through this instrument.In the past there were great movements inspired by the Avatars that brought certain truths to Earth. These gradually deteriorated over the centuries until only remnants of ritual and form remained, leaving what were primarily hollow shells. In the future there will be a rebuilding and renewal. The seeds are being planted now for the greatness that is to come. Out of the ashes of the past and the present will emerge the Phoenix of our future greatness in science, religion, art, education, agriculture and earth stewardship.

> *Out of the ashes of the past*
> *and the present will emerge*
> *the Phoenix of our future greatness.*

England will remain in spite of various land changes. Scotland, and Ireland will find the ancient Celtic stories and legends as a resource for a new science and spiritually-based technology. The keys are held in ancient, crystal embedded stones throughout the islands.

At Glastonbury an ancient portal to other worlds, indeed to Hell itself, is closed permanently. The souls trapped in this hell realm have been released and sent on to their next place of evolution.

The Avebury stones hold the history of all the extraterrestrial visitors that have ever come to Earth. Each stone holds a record of a different star system and the nature of its interaction with the Earth. For example, there is information on the whales and the dolphins, there is information on the presence of the dinosaurs and their study which is still going on today. There is information from the Pleiades and from Arcturus and Sirius.

The keys to the understanding and interpretation of the information will be released soon. A great University will grow up to house and study this information. Any stones that have been destroyed have only been removed after all the records had been retrieved and the work that was represented by those records was completed. There were no "accidents" here. It is a very ancient star port. It will be brought to a more visible and active role in the near future.

Britain has played a key role in Earth's history, from the time of King Arthur's attempt to unify the mini-kingdoms to the recent history of bringing British understanding of government around the world to the various countries under her dominion. Much has been learned and there is much still to be given to the world by Britain.

New Zealand will hold the Ray of Purity. The principle *Ascension Temple* will be located there. There will be five others around the planet eventually.

Egypt, long the holder of the ancient Atlantean mysteries, and the etheric location of the Ascension Temple at Luxor, is currently too near the volatility and unrest in the Middle East. This may require a full deactivation of the Great Pyramid, which is still only partially activated. No specific determination has been made yet.

The Great Pyramid and the Temples at Luxor will remain unusable until political and social unrest are cleared. Should there be a healing here—and it is not clear at this time if that is possible—the Great Pyramid and the Temple at Luxor have the potential to be used as in the past as great focuses of learning and a key space port. That use of the Pyramid that was made by the space beings of the past will be a definite potential of the future.

At the present time, the actual focus of the Ascension Ray is being held by Sai Baba in India, through a certain specific (also not to be named) location in India until a final stable location can be determined. His physical passing recently will not make a difference as he transcends such "details."

(Author's note: We feel called to make an update on the Avatar Sai Baba as there has been a significant change since 1997. The energies once held by him as a single individual have since been distributed through several individuals around the planet. These include several of his devotees and at least one young child that we are aware of. It is reported that there is a man in Canada who is now offering all the miracles and manifestations as well. We suggest that this will enable many more to experience the love and the blessings of the Presence of this being rather than focusing on the individual or human expression.)

Mother Amachi of India is also holding the great Mother Ray of Divine Love for the planet and assisting in anchoring the Ascension Ray.

Mother Meera in Germany, an incarnation of Divine Mother, is single-handedly holding the responsibility for the energy work of one of the key points that will ultimately be focused in the Ural Mountains. Regional political unrest makes this transfer impossible at this time and for the foreseeable future. The exact location of the physical point in Europe is not disclosed.

Mother Meera works also as part of the clearing of the abominations wrought by Hitler in Germany and Stalin in Russia. Both of these were under the influence of malign influences that have been cleared from Earth. Any remnants visible in expression such as Nazi groups, etc., are the result of lesser malign influences that were part of the larger and are part of the "mopping up" program now underway.

We would encourage you to know, despite your desire

for historical records, that the continued maintenance of the concentration camps, and other focus on the atrocities, are in fact part of the process which allows these energies to continue to perpetrate the horror. Obviously there are many factors here and we acknowledge that. However, when you are confronted by such horror, our recommendation is to turn away and use the frequencies of the Violet Flame to transmute and to forgive any and all thought forms that have been, are now or ever will be connected to it.

The Diamond Mines of South Africa are another key point in the Earth Matrix. It is actually a yet-to-be-discovered location where the focus is held at this time. This is the work of certain Lightworkers in the area and their links with the interstellar fleets. The contamination of the people of Africa through centuries of slavery, tribal wars, and Western greed has required intervention (of the space fleet) here, which is unusual, and the work will be transferred to humanity fully as soon as possible.

The abuses of which we speak have not created the kind of contamination that existed in India or Mexico, and hence the land is still viable for these cosmic purposes. We will not attempt to deal here with the effects of the abominations of Hitler and Stalin.

Mt. Shasta - Planetary Crown Chakra.

Mt. Shasta, in Northern California, is the single remaining power point on the Earth which is fully functional.

(Note: December, 2012 - This is still true, however over the next five years there will be major reactivations of the other nine chakras [yes, 9].

It serves now as the planetary crown chakra. Home of the Violet Ray of St. Germain. It is also temporarily serving as the anchor point for all the rays until the new patterns stabilize and the Teachers of the Wisdom are moved to the various temple locations in alignment with the main planetary chakras.

To this location are drawn those seeking to learn and to work at the highest levels currently available now on Earth. Here the sacred priesthood is being trained and activated collectively on both physical and inner levels.

From here will come the New Ray of Hope for humanity, anchored in the lives and Eternal Presences of those who serve here and those who bring their lessons to the World after their sojourn here.

In spite of their great service and attunement to the Light, the Lightworkers here need to attune more directly to the Heartbeat of the Earth. Their attunement to higher realms is so great that they are losing touch with Earth. Only a very few are holding their focus in full alignment with the Earth. This is imperative for the full realization of their missions.

We would point out that the focused effect of energy from Mount Shasta extends a full 100 miles in all directions. A variety of activities will be emerging in the surrounding areas due to these resonating frequencies which demand expression as their pulses quicken the life patterns of those in their field.

Bali - Temple of the Cosmic Christ

We have left the Bali Site until last, because it is to be the jewel in the lotus, the one point on Earth where love was best expressed. The Heart Center of the Earth will beat through Bali. Pink is the light of the New Dawn energies. Love is the frequency of Life. Here will emerge the Temple of Love in its truest splendor. Much will be revealed to those who come to Bali to Love and to worship the One.

A great star overlights this point. It will be the *Temple of the Cosmic Christ*. Many will be drawn here in years to come. Only those of the greatest love will be able to remain, but all will be touched who come to Bali.

Certain great stargates have been contacted through the Bali Matrix and have set the field and the focus here for the next 2,000 years.

In summary, we have:

Mt. Fuji - deactivated

Palenque - deactivated/closed

Mt. Kailash - deactivated

China - not to be spoken of, however prayer is always appropriate.

Egypt, Great Pyramid - may be deactivated pending developments; optional space port. Temple of the Sun possible at Luxor.

Planetary Chakras - most chakras are not being specified as 1st or 2nd, etc., at this time because of the ongoing changes on Earth.

Mt. Denali - root chakra, base note for the Earth

Dalai Lama's Ashram in Northern India (temporary) - Yellow Gold Ray of Enlightenment and Buddhic consciousness.

Bali - Heart Chakra - Pink Ray; Temple of Love.

Mt. Shasta - Seventh Ray of Transmutation, Fourth Ray of Ascension; all Rays (temporarily). One of the main spiritual universities on the Planet to be anchored here.

New Zealand - White Ray of Purity - Fourth Ray also, Hope and Ascension.

for good in the world and even change the weather.
But who would want that kind of responsibility? It's too much power. Right? Absolute power corrupts absolutely, right? Wrong!

Power without Love and Wisdom can be abused and lead to corruption. But this is the time to reclaim all of your power in the fullness of the Divine Plan—in balance with Divine Love and Divine Wisdom. Then, there is no separation between your will and Divine Will. You are not seeking your personal gain. Rather, in seeking the good of all, you find yourself included. This is Enlightened Self Interest.

Only by seeking to serve the highest good for all can we act in such a way that our own best interests are served as well. Oh, no! I hear you exclaim—isn't that the royal road to ruin followed by Hitler and his ilk.

Not at all. It is true that each (most of us) of us carry some pattern of distortion in our human personality. Giving away your power is not the solution. Feigning ignorance and powerlessness does not make a problem go away.

The only solution is to claim your power and the responsibility to choose at the highest level of your ability—to choose to act with the greatest integrity and vision you can achieve. Each step upward leads to another level of growth. Each step downward leads to destruction. Standing still is not an option. The Bible states it emphatically:"Because thou art lukewarm, and neither cold nor hot, I will spew you out of my mouth." (Revelations 1:15).

Native American traditions have included the power to call for rain or to send it away. Shamans and medicine men/women are well aware of what is required. Just about everyone has heard of rain dances.

The weather responds to the collective accumulation of physical, emotional and mental energies of the region. The great weather spirits—or devas—will either respond to that which is unconscious or to those who choose to communicate with them, to conscious commands from humanity.

Well, yes, if 10,000 conflicting requests for rain, sunshine and a hailstorm to punish an enemy arise, you do not get clear communication or good weather. It is more like random chance.

What does it take to direct the weather patterns effectively and responsibly, and why should we? Wouldn't that be interfering with God's will?

It is Divine Will that humanity claim its full power and authority in complete alignment with Truth and Love.

Power wielded without Love is a disaster. Denying your power leads to victimization and is not an answer either. Yes, there may well be mistakes as you learn to walk this path. This is why there must be a growing alignment with your own Divine Nature. That part of you which is One with All That Is knows what right action looks like. The powers that you will have available to you will be in proportion to your alignment with the Source.

> *It is Divine Will that humanity claim*
> *its full power and authority*
> *in complete alignment with Truth and Love*

The safety feature here is that actions produce reactions. There is cause and effect. Due to the increasing vibratory rate on the Earth, what you put out is coming back at you pretty fast. It used to take lifetimes. These days it can be a matter of hours or seconds.

There is now on Earth a higher percentage of the higher vibrational rays than we have been able to sustain before, and a smaller proportion of the lower vibrational rays. This has led to an overall increase in the Earth's vibratory rate.

What this leads to is manifestation of what you ask for

very quickly, and the consequences of any repercussions as well. When the simple principles are understood, no sane person would act in any way other than the highest they can imagine, because anything else will be in their face sooner than they want to know.

So, maybe you have absolutely no desire to have anything to do with changing the weather. O.K. Let us assume that this is your desire, your truth at this time. We bring this to your attention because someday that may change. You may need protection from a hurricane or rain for your garden some day.

These are the principles—if and when you need them or choose to use them:

♦ Call for the Presence and assistance of your Higher Self—Christ Self—Buddha Self—I Am Self—Mother/Father Self.
♦ Call for the overlighting Angel of the garden or region in question to be with you.
♦ Ask that what you request be only for the Highest Good of all concerned and in alignment with any factors of which you are not aware.
♦ Ask that all proceed in love, joy, harmony, peace and safety.
♦ State your request (you may state it as a command) in as clear and specific a manner as you wish. Conscious language is of value here. In Neal Donald Walsh's book, Conversations with God, Book I, God points out that to say "I want ..." means God gives you wanting. Try "I choose ... " or
"Thank you for bringing ..."
♦ Say thank you.
♦ Let it go.

Perhaps you only want your azalea bush or roses to do

better. Speak with the Azalea Deva or the Rose Deva. Perhaps you cannot hear what he/she says. Ask that the necessary information come to you in other ways and that you notice it when it does.

Does this mean that we can expect to see 10,000 people standing outside in the middle of a thunderstorm yelling for the rain to stop? Hopefully not. We would rather see that than 10,000 people living in ignorance, but we anticipate 10,000 or 10,000,000 people will learn to ask God, "What is your will here? What is the highest good for all?"

Can 10,000 or 10,000,000 directing their loving intention for balance, harmony and grace for the atmospheric conditions of the planet make a difference? What do you think?

We envision ten thousand or ten million people praying, consciously choosing, to send love and good intentions to the Angels and devas of the weather making a tremendous difference.

You do not need to try to send rain to the Sahara desert or to reverse the ozone layer disintegration. Merely ask that Harmony, Love, Joy and Peace permeate the atmosphere, freely available to the hearts and minds of all. Ask that rain be a blessing to the Earth and all life; that sun be a blessing; that distortion from collective pain, fear, rage be dissolved through the power of Love.

You have the power Now
to make a difference.

You have the Power now to make a difference. Choose to use your Power with Love and Wisdom in full alignment with Divine Will for the good of all. To those to whom much has been given, much will be expected.

Perhaps you will be one who feels called to work directly in the world as well, reclaiming land damaged or destroyed by pollution, healing lakes, rivers and water-ways or working to bring organic methods to farmers here or abroad.

Whatever your right livelihood looks like, there are steps that will take you there.

♦ Learning to listen to God.

♦ Asking for, praying for the highest good for all.

♦ Being willing to claim your personal Power and strength, balanced with Love and Wisdom.

♦ Loving yourself and all life enough to ask for what you need and expecting to get it.

♦ Learning to attune to the Earth and finding your right relationship to her.

♦ Learning to work in harmony, love and balance with all kingdoms: the elemental, human, and Angelic.

♦ Learning to work as an individual in alignment with the whole.

♦ Learning what you love, who you love, who you are, what you have to give.

♦ Allowing yourself to be the best that you can be, beyond family or cultural expectations—all the way to God's Vision of who you are.

And we point out to you, as well, in these troubled times, these principles work equally well when asking for health, harmony, peace and prosperity for the world. Pray for good decision making in government and business. Pray for healing for countries torn by war and natural disasters. Pray to link with all others of like intention so that one unified purpose might fill the planetary mind, rather than confused and conflicting ideas.

You have the Power Now
to make a difference.

Chapter Seventeen

Right Use of Power

Beloved Ones, I Am Sunanda.

W e will indeed speak of witchcraft today. Have we not been speaking of reclaiming your power? That which lies in the collective unconscious as a source of dread is the misuse of power, often mistakenly tied to witchcraft.

The practice of Wicca does indeed give one access to power. In past centuries, this has been seriously abused by some, certainly not by all.

It was during the Middle Ages, when the Church sought to be the sole source of power, good or bad–and there was much corruption within the Church at the time—that persecution of all that was outside the Church grew and flourished.

The barbarism, the tortures of the Middle Ages were horrific. It is no wonder that power has gained such a bad reputation.

Many sincere herbalists and healers were killed in the various witch hunts, but I say to you, make no mistake, the misuse of power is definitely a tool of evil. The greater the power that you access, the greater has been the testing by the dark forces to see if here was one who could be used.

However, one certainly doesn't have to have been a witch to have wielded power or abused it.

We are specifically speaking of witchcraft here because

there are so many who have dabbled in it over the centuries. And we see many today who are carrying much of this energy still in their auric fields.

As we have said, this is a time of choosing. We hope to have this be conscious choice for as many as possible.

Which aspect of the Goddess that is worshipped can be significant here. None who walked the dark paths remained unsullied because the distortion which has marred this universal expression made it impossible.

And yet, only by experiencing this distortion have we been able to understand it and find the means to clear it. And the clearing is nearly completed on Earth and all the galactic linkages that she represents.

We are going to be very specific here on this issue and how to clear any remaining traces you may hold—or others may be holding over you.

First, examine yourself in a mirror. Do you dress like a "traditional" witch. Do you wear a lot of black (or red) clothes? Is there a lot of black around your eyes or mouth?

This does not mean that you are currently practicing witchcraft (or black magic) or have any desire to do so. It is an indication, though, that you may have unresolved past lives. Even more significantly, those lives may be bleeding through into this one. It is entirely possible for such a past life presence to use their power to drain energy from you (and other life streams) in your current life.

It is imperative that these connections be cut and all of your power be reclaimed, brought into present time, and purified so that it may be used for your own purposes. We obviously hope that your choice is to use it for good. However, it is still your choice how you use it.

Many are being drawn to exploring Wicca these days. It may be primarily due to unresolved past life issues. There is also the desire of many women (and men) to really know

Conscious Self to Inner Child: You want to feel safe and loved, cared for and protected. Can Inner Lover take care of you? Yes (in a small voice). Say it louder, as if you mean it. YES. O.K. you go over right now and he will hold you. O.K? O.K. To the witch: Can you see other powerful women with sexy, wonderful men in their lives? Yes . . . Do you believe you deserve it? . . . Yes . . . Do you need to steal from someone else to have it? . . . No . . . Is there enough to go around? . . . Yes . . . How powerful do you want to be? . . . Very . . . How loving? . . . Max . . . Can we change your name and your image? . . . OK . . . How about Goddess? . . . Hmmm, I like that! I still feel powerful, oh yes! Sexy, umhmmm, loving, Very! OK. OK!

Inner Lover: Be at Peace, my jewel, all goes well. I will tell you when it is time.

Inner Mother: You deserve the best, dear. I will be sure that you are ready. The love you have to give will have its chance to be.

Inner Child: I guess it would be OK now.

Rebel: Well, as long as I can be myself! I can't live in a box.

Adventurer: There have been too many compromises and constraints already. I choose more freedom. I choose a fine, sturdy, good looking car. I choose a partner who is willing to play and grow and stretch and explore.

I Am Presence: You deserve the best. You are the best. Believe it. I Am bringing you everything you desire. Open up your arms and receive it now. Step out of the limitations of the past. See the door to the world you are choosing and step through now.

(Vision of a door opened wide, client steps through to be greeted by happy, joyful voices, laughter, a big party. There are friends there waiting to play.)

This scenario is not the only way the issues might have been resolved. Often it takes quite a bit of discussion to get some members of your team up to speed. Sometimes there *is quite a bit of contamination due to dysfunctional family experiences.*

If you don't feel confident in dealing with some of the more difficult members, ask if there is someone in the group (like the Higher Self) who can take them on.

(I, Mikaelah, once had a past life personality I was attempting to integrate and I didn't like him. I couldn't stand him! I thought he was completely hopeless: selfish, mean and ruthless. When I asked for help from my inner team, my inner child came up and took him by the hand. I was floored. An inner voice informed me: "Now, Mikaelah, nobody is all bad.")

Many of you have the life skills and experience to handle this exercise easily. Others of you readers will find this exercise entirely too new to do readily. Here is where some experienced help is handy. Even when you have lots of practice in these techniques, an objective helper can be very useful.

Those trained in such modalities as psychosynthesis, voice dialogue and Alchemical Hypnotherapy® will be able to help you with such a technique.

Counselors with training in transpersonal psychology will also be very valuable, as is a spiritual perspective. It still is necessary for you to choose someone with whom you have a good rapport. These techniques are very powerful and very fast, but the counselor or hypnotherapist must be sensitive to your needs as well as having the appropriate experience to help you best.

Chapter Twenty

Love and the
Avatar of Synthesis

Lord Jesus/Sunanda speaks:

Royalty in Heaven?

In heaven, rank or hierarchy is based on love—how much love you hold, and conversely, how much love you give. As you find the love you wish to share is more than you have available, then you move to a level where you can hold more and therefore give more.

Love is not based on higher than or lower than but on the desire to share. Thus, the more you give away, the more you have. In the Bible it is written, "you shall be given pressed down, overflowing " (Luke 6:38). Truly there is no limit to Love.

We find our hearts are drawn to that which is by its very nature Love. Why are millions drawn to Krishna, to Rama, Shiva, Jesus, Buddha, Quan Yin, Mother Mary, the Goddess? It is because we feel and experience their Love.

Love is the attraction energy of Life. From the tiniest subatomic particles, to men and women, gods and goddesses, that which is separate is drawn to one or more others to form that which is greater. That power to draw together is Love.

The Christ—the Avatar of Synthesis—is here to draw together through the power and the principles of Love and to create in Unity.

Is it not appropriate that this Avatar Principle is expressed in many forms working in Unity?

It is Love which has been the underlying Principle of all the great religions. And it is Love which will be the Unifying principle that will allow this Vision to move past all seeming barriers into Unity.

We call each of you now to see those barriers within your hearts and to call on the Angels and your Higher Self for assistance in removing them. It is time for Love to grow.

Exercise 20-1 Healing the Heart

Imagine a door into your Heart. Go with an Angel and a lamp to seek the corners and the crevices to look for that which is to be healed or cleared away. Let Love fill every place within your heart. Let your Heart be healed. It is time.

Take your time to do this carefully. The instructions are brief, but the experience may not be.

ଛୀଔ

Mikaelah was long ago given several visions which spoke to this truth of where we are going—of the unified consciousness. She will tell of them here in her own words.

The first vision that came to me was very early on in my conscious exploration of "the path" (around 1986). At the time I thought that perhaps visions such as these would be commonplace but I have since learned that they are rare and very precious.

I was shown people coming together in groups of seven and they were bonding much like the carbon atoms of a carbon ring are bonded.

In a carbon ring, carbon atoms come together and form a cohesive and stable ring because of the strength of the chemi-

cal bonds. All of the proteins and complex carbohydrates that make up the cells, organs, hormones and plants and physical

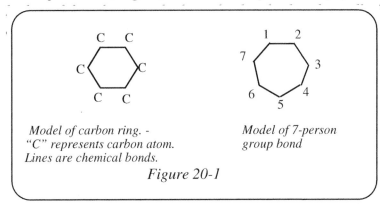

Model of carbon ring. -
"C" represents carbon atom.
Lines are chemical bonds.

Model of 7-person
group bond

Figure 20-1

The idea of moving from six to seven seemed significant to me and I thought that perhaps it was indicative of whole new levels of creation becoming possible.

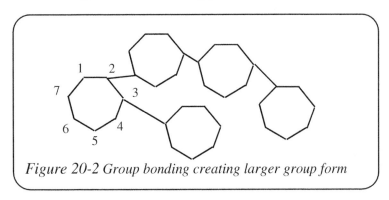

Figure 20-2 Group bonding creating larger group form

I then saw that bonds would form from each of the individuals at the center and create complex relationships such as might be perceived in complex proteins built on the framework of the carbon ring. In this instance, though, the relationships built would be human and the bonds those of love.

I understood this to be the building of the Body of God (or the Body of Christ) on our planet. We are ready to participate in co-creation with God on an unprecedented level.

A collective consciousness is emerging which is built on each of us as individuals.

Barbara Marx Hubbard speaks of this evolutionary leap as we build the body of God in her many books envisioning the future. The group Global Family developed workshops and training materials which articulate this very beautifully.

I received this vision at about the same time that group was formed, which indicated to me that people all over the planet were receiving variations of this construct. Others are developing their pieces in the larger puzzle that is coming together.

I saw this mixing together of individuals in various groups in chemical terms. These groups would work for a while and then dissolve, truly in a similar manner in which chemical catalysts are combined with various ingredients to assist in forming complex compounds. Some compounds are very temporary or unstable and are only a brief step in the process that leads to a final result.

Since that vision, I have participated in a number of groups where new bonds were formed among us, a new level of group consciousness was formed, and then for the most part, the groups dissolved and the individuals went on to repeat this process with other groups.

In some groups the cohesion-bonding was almost instantaneous: one gathering, love shared, never to meet again. In other groups we met for weeks or months exploring whether we could overcome our personality differences, our rough edges and prickly exteriors. Sometimes we did, allowing love to win. At other times, it did not seem possible.

Each of these groups seemed to reach a point of no return. Often, in groups that worked, we would have the experience of a great flood of light and blessing. (I interpreted this as a group initiation taking us to a higher level of consciousness both as a group and as individuals.) Whether the group "jelled" or not, after this point the groups soon dissolved and we went our own ways.

The second vision I have been asked to share is one that I received only a few years after the first. Both were received while I still lived in Berkeley in the late 1980's. In this vision I was shown many different New Age groups moving past their differences and boundaries and really honoring each other. This was rapidly followed by various Christian groups dropping their artificial boundaries based on doctrinal differences and honoring the universal truths they each hold and the central figure of Christ around which they are all in harmony. This was part of a larger pattern of coming together and honoring one another that touched all religions and spiritual teachings. It culminated in a single day of world praise of God and of thanksgiving, marked by song, celebration and honoring of all traditions and praising God by all the world's diversity.

What will it take for this to come to pass?

I have watched the world and its dances, and I wonder. There are many moments that lead us to hope. The spectacle of round-the-clock/round-the-world celebrations on January 1, 2000 might be seen as a precursor of this other event. I hold these visions in my heart, and I wait and I watch.

2002 update: The planetary shockwaves that followed 9-11-2001 destruction of the World Trade Center and the Pentagon have precipitated movement in this direction. The prayer ceremony held at the National Cathedral in remembrance of those who died and those who mourned was televised world wide. and the Reverend Billy Graham spoke words of unity across religious boundaries, rather than words of separation.

2008 Comment: More recently, there were certainly world celebrations following the election of Barak Obama as President of the United States of America.

৩০৫

Chapter Twenty One

Peace

Mother-Father God Speak:

Beloved Ones, we speak to you of today and of that tomorrow of which you are so often concerned.

Be at peace about your tomorrows, beloved, for they grow surely from the fruits of your labors today.

It is this day that we ask you to be aware of and to be aware within. All your hopes and fears of the future must have their foundation in the present.

Beloved Ones, be at Peace. It is in the fields of Peace that you will create the Heaven you desire. Indeed, it is in the fields of Peace that Heaven will create itself around you.

For all that can be, or might be, or will be, exists in its potential right now. When you allow yourself a time of Peace, that which is in alignment with your greatest good comes to you easily and naturally. The world falls into place for you—so to speak.

Peace is an active principle

Peace is not just a cessation of war, beloved ones. Peace is an active principle. It represents the fulfillment and the balancing of all the other rays. The color of Peace is iridescent gold. It is all around you, and yet only when you allow the fears to still, the thoughts to quiet, the desires to rest, can you experience it.

Chapter Twenty Three

Creating Our Tomorrows

Beloved Ones, I Am the Christ.

I speak to you as the Christ of your heart. Truly, I say unto you, there is no separation. We are One.

Ever have I lived within you—awaiting this time of awakening, this time when all might know consciously and directly the joy of our union.

I ask that you allow the Truth which I speak to gently penetrate the layers of pain with which you have struggled for lifetimes. I have always been with you. Always!

I have always been with you. Always!

In fear and confusion you have closed the doors of your hearts. Your ears and eyes were closed to my words and my Light. But now, the long winter of separation is over. The Spring of our renewal and Resurrection is here. Awaken! Throw wide the doors of your inner vision and inner knowing. See me. Hear me. I Am with you.

Because the veils of illusion are dissolving, because the planetary shift in frequency makes our alignment easier than it has been for thousands of years, I call you each by name—the true name of your soul.

Awaken. Be with me now in full consciousness of the Glory that together We Are.

I ask you now to call on the Angels of Healing and all Divine Beings dedicated to assisting you at this time to your own Resurrection in the Light—your own Ascension into Conscious Unity with the Great I Am That I Am.

𝔊reat 𝔍 𝔄m 𝔗hat 𝔍 𝔄m

Sit quietly now. Call the Angels. Release the limitations and confusions of the past. Right now—in this moment— step out of your old garments that are tattered and frayed. They no longer serve you. Perhaps they served the ways of death. They do not serve the Life that now flows through the veins and arteries of this great Earth nor of the fleshly bodies that you wear—each a part of the whole.

Release these tattered remnants—reach out your hands and receive the garments of Light—that the Angels now offer you.

You are being bathed in Light. The auric layers of your Being are cleansed and purified in the Love that you have chosen.

Put on your garments of Light, woven by your words and deeds of Love. The time has come. You are ready. The world is ready, Now! There is no future date that will be better. I call you to full remembrance of who you are—Who We Are Now!

I call you to full remembrance
of who you are—Who We Are—Now!

Perhaps you have worked in my vineyards all your life. Perhaps you have only recently come—and worked only a few brief hours or days in my fields. Nonetheless, I choose to pay all the same. All receive the Grace of my Love in equal measure.

scribe it to you. It appeared as a very thin sheet of cloud. What made it stand out was the shimmering rainbow of colors that played over its surface on a clear, sunny day.

But, Jesus is already here with you now as well. He is on Earth in quite a number of human bodies.

Author's comment: I cannot tell you how many I have met. I lost track after I had counted 50 or so that I had personally met of these individual aspects and embodiments of Jesus. Many of these already knew or suspected it. Others were in denial.

One to whom I spoke said , "I always thought I was Jesus—I just never believed it." It seems a sad commentary on our society. If you think you are Jesus, you might as well say you are crazy, too.

But really, what does it mean that Jesus is here in many bodies?

First, it is in answer to the call of many hearts. The longing of a mother to know what it must have been like to carry that Baby, to nurture those precious years. The desire to have lived with, walked with, talked with Him has called that into many people's experiences.

> *What we focus on,*
> *what we love, we become.*

And yet, have we recognized it? Did you know that this man or woman who seemed so good and gentle, so loving and alive, carried the Spirit, the Soul, the Essence of Jesus?

If the longing of your heart to see Him, to know Him, to love Him is strong, He could be you. For what we focus on, what we love, we become. Does this seem sacrilegious? It is, rather, the Essence of Truth.

Why else is Jesus here in many bodies, both male and female? Because it is part of His growth and expansion as a

Divine Being to be in multiple forms simultaneously.

Finally, it is the nature of the Cosmic Christ to be a collective Principle—a unified field—of Christ Consciousness within which each individual shines in their uniqueness. Therefore, it may be helpful to understand the Second Coming as expressing in a three-fold manner:

♦ The reappearance of the individual, historical Jesus on a "cloud of glory" perhaps as the Bible says or with some variation.

♦ Many varied and unique expressions of the Christ Presence through many current bodies now on Earth, both male and female. These might be known as aspects, and each will hold varying percentages of that Presence according to their attunement as well they will be anchoring the Christ energies on many different dimensional levels according to their purpose, their Divine Plan and their personal spiritual evolution.

♦ The collective Christing of Earth as all humanity is overshadowed by the consciousness of the Cosmic Christ and one unified Christ Conscious Being is birthed.

> *The "Christing" of the Planet*
> *is about embodying and*
> *expressing Loving Essence.*

The "Christing" of the planet is *not* about practicing a particular religion. It is about embodying and expressing Loving Essence.

In the largest sense, we are all expressions of God—of Love. And we each have our spiritual lineage—our gifts and talents, our rays, our alignment with various Divine expressions and various starry homes that make up our individuality.

We are aware that there are still some of you who may not relate to the name Jesus or the term "the Christ." A variety of human experiences may have led to this, or the call of your heart, may be to Buddha, the Divine Mother, Nature, or a rejection of any kind of religion or spiritual practice at all. This does not keep you from practicing and expressing Loving Essence. It is Love which is the common denominator for those who will participate in the planetary Christing.

Exercise 24-1: Healing religious pain

For those of you to whom the term "Christ" or the name "Jesus" gives pain or anger, we ask you to forgive those who have caused you pain or injury through their ignorance. After all, "Not all who say Lord, Lord, shall enter the kingdom of heaven." (Matthew 7:21).

There is a part of each of you that carries these wounds. Please take a moment to heal every record, memory, pattern or trace of negativity that you might carry from any lifetime.

"Ask and ye shall receive." Close your eyes and allow your breath to carry your thoughts into your heart and ask for your heart to release the pain you have carried. Ask to forgive and be forgiven. Ask that your mind and heart be healed fully, here and now. Ask your Angels and your Higher Self to be with you and to help. Ask the Angels of the Violet Flame to purify and transmute all the memories and all the pain.

Please forgive those who have unintentionally harmed you thinking it was somehow pleasing to God. Please forgive those whose ignorance led them to act in ways that did not demonstrate the Love that is the essence of the teachings of Jesus and the Presence of the Christ. Please forgive any and all in this lifetime and all lifetimes; this world and all worlds, this reality and all parallel realities, this universe and all alternate universes.

Please allow yourself to be freed from past programming

that has made it difficult or impossible to open to this Love. For the Christ is the Love that is in all things.

Please extend this forgiveness to all spiritual or religious wounds. Allow perfect Love to cast out all pain and all fear. Accept the lessons that have come to you through these experiences. Acknowledge your essential wholeness now.

Perhaps you would like to meet with Jesus and speak to him of the wounds you or those you cared about received and to forgive and to be forgiven for all misunderstandings of the past.

Exercise 24-2 Healing Archetypes of Father and Mother and Generational Patterns.

And there are wounds associated with God as Father and God as Mother. Again, ask your Angels, your Higher Self, the Holy Spirit, the One—whatever term works for you—for healing body, emotions, mind and spirit. Forgive your Mother and your Father, both heavenly and earthly. Ask to be forgiven. The commandment "Honor your Father and your Mother" calls for the healing of those patterns of distortion that you may have experienced, so that wholeness of the Feminine and the Masculine Principle could be restored, both in you, in the Earth, and in this Universe.

In healing the issues of Mother and of Father, we replace the possible distorted images that we acquired from our Earthly parents or role models. We free ourselves to take on the patterns of perfection reflected in the Divine Archetypes. No longer must we listen to the critical parent repeating negativity or cultural stereotypes through our subconscious. We can retire these beings from our inner councils. Release the pain and the anger and set yourself free.

We not only have permission, but we have the Divine Imperative to reunite with our Divine Parents and to begin to hear messages of love, support, strength, reassurance and wisdom in the inner realms of mind and heart.

We have the Divine Imperative to Reunite with our God Parents.

Allow yourself and your inner child to meet with your own unique expression of Divine Mother. Feel her arms holding and comforting you. Hear her words of love and support. Let the tears flow and the anguish release.

Again allow yourself and your inner child to meet with your own personal experience of the Divine Father. Feel his strength, integrity and wisdom. Let him hold you and comfort you.

What are the precious gifts that these parents offer you. Meet with them regularly in your meditation time. Let their voices become your source of inner strength, solace and wisdom. Let their love sustain you daily, hourly, moment by moment.

Whose voice to you choose to hear? Does it serve you to hear the voices of your earthly parents? Or would you be better served by Divine Parents? A Divine Mother is one who can love and nurture you as you are and who represents the true feminine nature. A Divine Father who gives you the attention, strength and protection you need and represents all that is finest in the masculine pattern.

Allow the voices that speak to be those of your true inner parents. Free yourself now from the chains of the past—of imperfect parenting, however well intended.

Bless your parents; forgive them. Release them from your subconscious programs. Claim your Divine Heritage Now! Invite new Divine parents to heal and nurture your inner child and to create a new inner template of the best of the Masculine and Feminine.

You took on your life experiences so distortion could be examined and corrected. Have you not looked at the patterns of your life? Have many of you not said, "My God, this has been going on for generations. No more. The buck stops here! My life, my children's lives will be different."

You can use the Violet Flame to transmute these family and generational patterns. See in your mind's eye the images that relate to these patterns, the thoughts and feelings, the pain and the sorrow. Ask that all the generations that are connected to this pain and this pattern release from you and your entire genetic lineage into the Violet Flame. Release it from you, from your family and from all who might have ever suffered from these distorted patterns.

Next take a moment to allow your soul to give you the idea of the highest and the best that might have been.

Hold this thought in your mind's eye and in your heart. Send this thought as a prayer or as a blessing to the collective consciousness of the earth.

Take a moment and breathe the very breath of Mother-Father God into this holy vision of what can be—of what will be. Allow the Peace and the feelings of rightness, Love and Beauty to fill you as you hold this thought for all humanity.

And when you are ready, release it to the universe and bring your attention back to your physical self as you are right now. Take a few more deep breaths and open your eyes into the present moment, feeling clearer and freer, ever sustained in the Love of God.

isn't exactly that everyone is impoverished. Let's say the economy has downsized—a lot. People are learning to live a lot more simply. A lot less meat in the diet for one. Mass contamination of the food supply keeps people focused on healthy foods, and organic suppliers are preferred.

There is a lot of instability and uncertainty in the world. Your friend Mary is living in Hawaii. A community has grown up around her and her teachings. She has a lovely place on Kauai.

2017—. *(Please do the same exercise for yourself first.)*

2017 Self - A very deep peace fills me. The world is very quiet.

Many have left. It is a time of renewing and replenishing of the Earth.

By 2014 so much had happened, you could hardly believe it. Massive numbers of people left. After the space ships started landing regularly, many just wanted to go home. There were years of attunement gatherings. People had to acclimatize to the new ways. But the leaders were so charismatic, many were attracted to work and learn so that they could join their communities. The soul connections were tremendous.

It was strange to see how many wanted to go. Of course, Earth has definitely had her share of difficulties, but still it is a very beautiful place.

It will be a few years, still, before the new colonists begin arriving for the resettlement phase. Earth shifts are requiring a longer delay than was originally expected.

My family is still here with me, but we will be leaving soon ourselves. We are going to Venus. I am signing up for some major rejuvenation treatments and then I will decide what to do next. There is the possibility of a speaking tour. Many want to hear what happened on Earth.

In the last years the love was incredible. You could hardly imagine what was going on from where you are today. Poverty just disappeared. People got so good at listening to what was right for themselves, that sharing and flow were effortless. There was so much joy, so much singing and laughter. I can't really describe it to you very well.

2047—The world almost seems reborn. The light levels are incredible. Rainbows glimmer in the trees, in the water. In the skies it is like the Aurora Borealis all the time—well, frequently.

There are a few native groups that elected to stay on as caretakers of various regions. They were provided with climate-controlled, safe environments for the transition times and then they were free to relocate wherever they wanted.

It was decided that Peace must be allowed to reign supreme. The plans for interplanetary headquarters and such are on hold for now. No one can bear to interfere just yet with the Beauty and the Peace that rest as a healing balm over all. Soon, now, there will be some selected teams arriving. They will determine if it is yet time to begin "growing" the new cities.

These will be grown in full communion with the elemental kingdom. Certain ones of Earth have been training off planet to implement this phase.

Most of the animal populations are gone for now. There will be some re-seeding in alignment with the new patterns. Right now, Peace reigns supreme.

It will be several thousand years before the Earth is once again filled with life.

The old cities are to be destructured—the core elements of the buildings will be returned to the Earth. There will not be centuries of decay; they will just be gone.

2097—The new cities are emerging very artfully. Highly harmonized teams of artists, musicians, architects and planners are working together with the elementals and overlighting Angels of the regions to create incredible spaces for living, working and co-creating. The cities are created with music and vision and the cities grow on the vibration of sacred sound.

The Earth is a vast university. The students come here from everywhere to learn of the wonders of co-creation in harmony with all. The diversity that is her strength continues to be a unique contribution to consciousness for all who come here from throughout the universe.

I sit in slightly shocked awe as these words come to me. It takes me several weeks to process this information.

The next morning, I remember a dream which seems directly related to the above information so I include it and my interpretation as well.

I was on the 2nd floor of a large hospital, Ward 2E. Some children were playing near an elevator. Two suddenly squealed as they fell down the shaft. They only fell two or three feet. But the door was shut now and they couldn't be extricated. We were going to need help to rescue them. I couldn't get anyone on the phone. It seemed as though there might be some kind of emergency. People in wheelchairs were gathered to see if there was to be an evacuation.

I volunteered to go downstairs to the administration offices and get more information. When I arrived, there were hundreds of people leaving the building. It was as though a large class or workshop had just completed. All the participants had given each other these wonderful handmade cards covered with roses. Some looked like miniature rose gardens.

I talked with one of the staff—a woman—and asked her whether we needed to evacuate. Was there an emergency? "Oh, no," she said, "everything is all right." When I asked her what was going on, she turned to a colleague to discuss exactly how to explain it. I also told her about the problem with the children in the elevator shaft.

Meanwhile, I decided to return to the 2nd floor (against the flow of traffic, which was thinning a bit) and told everyone—there were even more people gathered—15 or 20 by now in wheelchairs and on crutches— that they could go back to bed. There was no need to evacuate. If anything changed, they would be notified.

I woke up.

Interpretation: Those who had graduated, completed their courses were leaving. The roses given to one another were symbolic of the love that they were expressing.

Those who were wounded seriously could go back to bed, representing, stay in the unawakened state, as well as the need for further rest and healing.

We weren't told all that was happening. Those in charge were still deciding how to describe it to us.

2E - E could represent Earth, both a hospital and a classroom. Two represented duality. The wounded who weren't ready to leave on their own would be taken care of as they were accustomed to. Their need for healing and rest would be taken care of.

The children in the elevator shaft represented a message to me (and possibly the reader as well) about certain projects that seemed to have been lost, but merely needed some help to rescue them from the elevator shaft. They were just fine. Unharmed in every way, just inaccessible for the moment.

There is a lot happening just now, but it is all being taken care of. It isn't necessary to leave now.)

(Author's update: in May of 2002 I began a new look as some of this had happened, some had not, some was still to be determined.

My future self speaks from 25 years into the future: Beloved, I Am your Future Self. Allow me to describe what is happening. The Earth has divided itself. It was not what was desired, but too many did not choose to move forward. Those who attempted to control circumstances to their liking actually forced the world into convolutions that never needed to happen. Many bought into the reality that was presented to them.

Then, as I looked, I saw absolutely nothing. I didn't know what this meant, but I was very frightened. So frightened that I turned away from the book and my work and buried myself in reading novels (my form of escape). It was several months later, that I realized that some part of me, all too human, had run from this vision and I turned again to my inner Self. This next part was written then.

July, 18, 2002: I seriously did not want to look at what I was seeing here. A world that was not my ideal. So, I spent nearly two months avoiding it and pretending I had never heard the words nor seen the visions. Perhaps I am ready now to accept what I see and hear and to record it.

Beloved, I Am Sunanda. Yes, there are many things that are not right with the world. At the same time, there is much that is real and very, very beautiful. What is to be the focus here, that which is ugly, painful and sordid, or that which is ideal?

Here we are faced with a dilemma. Look on and give reality to the sordid and the ugly, or focus only on the ideal and somehow ignore the pain and sorrow in the world. How does one create the future in the face of a present that seems to be self destructing.

Remember to Breathe

First, beloved, remember to breathe. Remember that we are co-creating our reality with God and one another. Focus first on the local reality, that which is in your immediate vicinity. What do you desire?

Remember, these visions of the future represent just one possible reality. Things might happen this way or not. Even one or two people making their choices might significantly alter key factors which could affect millions. Princess Diana's death is an example of one person's choices having an international impact on our choices and perspectives collectively.

Other people, less well known, can have just as significant an impact through seemingly simple choices. We are all connected through the vast web of life.

The most important thing to do today is to live here and now, to be fully present. Deal consciously and lovingly with what is needed today—this moment.

For at least ten years, we can expect things to appear much the same.

It is not time to throw away your lives and go wait on a mountain top for a spaceship to come and whisk you away. Only by being fully present, living here now, with the greatest Love, Joy, Peace, and Wisdom you can, will you be ready to go at all.

Let us be the best we can be here and now. The future will arrive at its own pace and with its own needs. The best preparation is to take care of your life as it is today. Speculation will not serve us, especially not if it leads you away from being fully present to the needs and choices of today.

These were my visions. I would be interested in hearing what others see. Perhaps another book can be created of these alternate perspectives.

This is a good time to remember the story of the five blind men and the elephant. Each man touched a different part of the elephant. One touched an ear and declared an elephant to be like a large leather fan. A second touched the trunk and declared an elephant to be like a large hose. A third stood by a massive leg and said, "no, it was more like a tree trunk." The fourth touched the side and declared it was most like a wall. The fifth was near the tail and said, "not in the least, it is just like a whip."

We are each limited in our perspectives. By bringing our visions together we can get the clearest picture. Share your ideas with others, especially those who have a different perspective. Expand your vision if you want to see the larger picture.

(Author's comment: As an update report on the future, I am now three and one-half years into the future (2000) from these visions. Some of what I was told, has not happened as expected. Most of it is still in the wait-and-see phase.

I interpret this in the following way. First, my free will is making choices continually and appears to be quite able to create an alternative for me.

Second, what I saw was a personal future as well as a global future. Some parts of what I saw have been seen by others. Most of what I saw simply hasn't happened yet.

What I want to convey here is that our visions of the future are not set in concrete.

But I still believe that we will see the visitors from space and the rainbows across the planet someday.

2008: And as a further and final comment, I notice that I am currently living in apartment 2E and all my little children (my projects) are coming out of the elevator shaft and emerging to be in full flower. I am interpreting this as more signs that the Tribulation is over and we are out from under the darkness that was allowed its time of testing and is now receding.

In fact, so many good things are happening, it is my biggest task to to find balance in my life and allow time for rest, play and spending time with friends and family.

So, I encourage you to step joyfully into the future that is now emerging. It is good and will just get better.

80C8

Life is good and will just get better.

Chapter Twenty Seven

New Garments of Light

September 19, 2002

I *awoke to the presence of Love filling my heart and I heard the words "sixty seven."*

"Who is this?" I asked. "Are you my future self, when I am 67 and the year is 2012?" Words of assurance caused me to get up and to retrieve my notebook to record these words.

Beloved, I Am indeed your future self. We would speak here of the future which you so long for and of which you are simultaneously afraid to know.

Something good has happened. It has happened across the planet. Yes, we speak of your present, for it has significantly affected the future.

The words of Patricia Cota Robles which so resonated in your heart are indeed true. The most wounded souls of humanity (some call them the laggards) have chosen to remain with the Earth in her Ascension. The possible reality of needing two Earths, one to remain in third dimensional reality and one to move forward is not necessary now. The Light has won a significant victory within the hearts and minds of those who doubted, those who feared, those whose anger and shame, held them in patterns of darkness and negativity—lost in a world of their own self-destruction.

We ask that all who read these words take a moment now and say a prayer of thanksgiving for this achievement.

Thank yourself for your years, for your lifetimes of love and dedication—most especially for this lifetime and all the ways in which you gave of yourself despite the seeming difficulties of your situation.

Beloved ones, individually and collectively you have passed through the "eye of the needle." (From the words of Jesus when he said, "it is more difficult for a rich man to enter into heaven than for a camel to pass through the eye of the needle" [Matthew 19:24]. *This referred to a gate into Jerusalem which was so called because it was so low that camels had to virtually crawl through the space, and if they were packed high with goods, it made it even more difficult.*)

Even now, in the throes of the Tribulation, you have marched steadfastly onward, holding your intention, seeking to find ways of greater Truth, greater Beauty, greater Love.

And give thanks to God/Goddess/All That Is and all the Angels for the Love and Grace that held this beloved planet and all within it in a vision of Victory over sin, disease and death.

The time of the final Transition is fast approaching and we wish to caution you, "there is much still to be done."

Those who have chosen to awaken in these "latter days" must be given every assistance as they clear the pain and negativity of the past and daily step forward into greater and greater achievement, greater and greater Light.

Claim the Next Step in This Victory

We wish to honor each of you for all the gifts you have given and the challenges you have met and overcome, even for those times when it seemed one step forward and two steps back. Still you picked yourself up, looked long and hard at what had created limitation, and again stepped forward with love and determination to press onward to the goal—onward to Victory!—onward to greater and greater Love—onward to greater and greater Light—onward to greater and greater union with your Own Divine Presence.

We congratulate you and we issue a call to claim the next step in this Victory.

"What?" you might ask. "What is this step?" It is the step of fully claiming the Power and Authority of your Divinity. That Power and Authority is to be used to co-create with your own God-Self and with one another in harmony with All Life. Begin now to hold your part of the Vision of the New Golden Age and come together to share your visions and to plan and work together to bring them into form. Take one step at a time, in full union and full harmony with God in Heaven, Goddess on Earth and All Life in all levels of creation. Know as your deepest Truth that we are all One Being—never separate. As we Live and Move and Have our Beingness in that certainty of Oneness, we will always act to benefit the whole, knowing that the greatest good for all best serves each of us as individuals as well.

We further encourage you with the words of Swami Beyondananda, "Take time for more television. It is time to tell-a-vision."

It is Time to Tell-a-Vision

Let the whole world take heed and indeed be lifted up as the impact of these visions sweep the Earth and further lift the hearts and minds of all who see and hear them. And welcome the reappearance of Hope back in your hearts.

In a famous Greek myth, Pandora opened a forbidden box and all the troubles of the world escaped. She slammed it shut, but it was too late. In her haste, though she trapped one saving grace inside—that was Hope.

Open that box once again and allow the Angels of Hope to be released and come to each of you to fill you with Hope. Breathe it in. Allow it to restore your hearts and minds. Receive it and accept it, for it is as Real and as True as these words we speak to you.

Hope, remember is the Divine counterpart of Gabriel. Their Ray is Purity and Ascension. They lead us all forward into that next level of life. Receive the gift of Hope now. Allow your true purity and innocence to be restored. Wash in the waters of forgiveness and purification and step forward to receive new garments of Light. Enter now into your eternal Home. Step through these portals of Light—the Gates of Heaven are open. We welcome you Home.

Sit with these words. Take them in—one thought at a time. Allow yourself to receive and experience perfectly that which these words represent. Take all the time you need. Our Love is ever with you.

Mikaelah is coming to know herself as one with God, just as you are. So, these words, which come from her future self are the words of her Higher Self expressing through her as an ever-expanding vehicle of Light and of Love.

Be at Peace my Beloved Children of the Most High. May you know the depth and breadth and heights of Peace. Peace Be with You.

Peace Be with You.

I Am the Elohim Peace. I speak to you today in thanks for the many prayers from people all over the Earth which have allowed us to release unto you the Grace of Peace that you have so earnestly and steadfastly requested. We give thanks! It is so done.

May Peace forever reign on Earth as in Heaven.

Amen. Selah.

And now Lord Sunanda will speak with you.

Blessed and Beloved Children of Peace, pray that all might be made ready to enter the Kingdom of Love. Pray that all fear be dissolved in the white Light of the Christ. Pray that the realms of Paradise might be made manifest in your daily lives. Pray that you might know God as your personal friend, lover and redeemer,
> As Mother and Father,
> As Sister and Brother,
> As Friend and Lover,
> As Neighbor and Stranger,
> And always as Love.
Pray that all error might be healed and
> forever cleared from our world,
> from our thoughts, memories and desires.
Pray for the Perfect Manifestation
> of Divine Will on Earth,
> For Peace,
> For Grace,
> For Love,
> For Joy,
> For Harmony,
> For Wisdom,
> For Health,
> For Sharing and Caring,
> For Forgiveness, until all are past the need
>> for forgiveness, and everything
>> is recognized as perfect,
> For Gratitude.
Peace be unto you All beings of Love. Ye are Love incarnate. Know yourself and live the fullness of that Love. Call for the Angels. Speak words of Peace. Bless all who spitefully use you.

Is Love enough?

Jesus was a New Age teacher. Two thousand years ago he ushered in the New Piscean Age. Those who represented the organized religion of the day (Judaism) feared Him, claimed that He blasphemed, that He worked miracles through the power of the devil.

Today He has come again in many forms. Again He ushers in a New Age. Again those of organized religion fear Him, claim that She/He blasphemes, that He/She works miracles through the power of Satan.

Will it be ever thus?

Can Love rise Supreme at Last and Shine so that the Light of God is seen and known for what it is?

Can we see God in our friends and neighbors? Can we see Love acting in the world and call it by its own True Name?

Is it possible?

Is Love enough?

Is it enough for you?

Over money, fame and power?
Over safety and security?
Over limited views of good?
Can we give thanks to God for All things?

Please remember:

Love your neighbor as yourself.
For God so loved the World that He gave His only Son.
Give thanks in All things.
I Am the Way, the Truth and the Life.
Forgive seventy times seven.
Peace be unto you.

I Am Sunanda,
Lord of the Sun.
God of All Creation.
One with Jesus, the Cosmic Christ, Lord of All

Epilogue

As I am preparing this book for reprinting, many things have shifted in my life and in the world.

I see that there are some present difficulties that had been predicted moving rapidly across the planet. Many people with formerly secure lives and straightforward paths have found that the economy has shifted and left them on a foundation of shifting sands. Many people are in bankruptcy and others are losing their homes to foreclosure. Rising gasoline prices are affecting every part of our lives. We are being encouraged yet again to live more simply and again to live in faith that indeed we are cared for perfectly and all of our needs will continue to be met.

In spite of the difficulties of many, my own life is moving forward in ways I'd given up on. After ten years away, I am again living in Mount Shasta. My own work is expanding and moving forward almost miraculously. Projects that were put aside (fell down that elevator shaft) 8-10 years ago, are being brought back to light and ready to have a new life.

I was a last minute guest on a television program recently and I found myself telling the Lightworkers of the world that it was time for us all to dust off the old projects that were sitting on the shelf and bring them and themselves back into center stage. The Tribulation is over and the next phase of our work is emerging with great vigor and delight.

I find that I am not so interested in trying to see into the future, but that I am very much interested in really being present to my life, to the people I interact with daily, and to the world around me. The words of this book have been absorbed and are leading me forward with joy.

My friend Pat reported that she has started re-reading the book and is getting even more insights from it this time.

I feel incredibly blessed each day and I bless each of you in turn.

Several years ago a new type of energy work emerged for me and I have had the extreme blessing of being able to assist others to anchor new levels of their Higher Selves and to align with new levels of their Divine Plan. This work is called the **Star Nation Light Body Activation** and is just incredible.

I am presently working on two more books (in addition to the one that follows)

The first is a book for children brought to you with the cooperation of the elemental kingdom. *Shamus the Leprechaun* meets two children and teaches them simple and powerful tools and light techniques to heal and change their lives. It is powerful, precious and delightful.

The next is a work in progress called *"The Christing of Planet Earth."* It is in some ways mirroring the process of the Earth herself as the changes and the challenges continue.

And most unexpectedly, I am now hosting a television show called **Treasures of Mount Shasta**, focusing on Mount Shasta's sacred places of beauty and the spiritual teachers, artists, musicians and authors who are recognized around the world. I have had the privilege of working with the most amazing and beautiful people on my spiritual path and it is a delight to share them with you.

My website **www.mcordeo.4t.com** will offer information and links to the dvds of these programs and links to other teachings from these tremendous teachers, and some special messages for the coming days from Adama, High Priest of Telos and from Our Lady of Guadalupe.

There is much that is miraculous and wonderful happening as we release the past patterns and old paradigms. It can be challenging and it can be delightful. I remind you to pray daily for the healing and blessing of all life as our planet and all life transform, ascend and awaken.

God bless you all.   *Mikaelah Cordeo*

From the upcoming book

Honor Your Mother

by Mikaelah Cordeo

Mary, Mother of Us All

I Am Mother Mary.

I come to you as your personal Divine Mother.

To all who call to me, I Am there for them. Only if you turn your head away and close your eyes will I seem to be gone. Always I Am here. My Presence resides in the limitless realms of perfection.

When you lift your eyes above the denser levels of experience—into the pure, the true, the beautiful, the loving, you will find me there, waiting to enfold you in my loving arms, to kiss away your tears and fears, to heal and to bless.

I send Angels to watch over you.

Not all earthly difficulties can be changed, but your experience can be one of blessing, peace, healing and love if you pray for my Assistance.

Just as you knew Jesus as the Son of God—One with the Father—know Me as part of the Divine Family.

I offer this prayer to my Beloved Children throughout the world.

Peace of the Mother

Peace be unto you.
May your eyes ever focus
    on that which is true and beautiful.
May your hearts open wide
    as the wonders of the Universe
    are made manifest to you.
May the joyful songs of Angels
    fill your hearts and minds.
May your hands be tools of the Divine Principle
    which rules Heaven and Earth—
    blessing, healing, serving always.
May your feet ever walk the paths of Love,
    Wisdom and Divine Will.
May your Soul know its own True Nature and
    express Divinity's Gifts with Grace and Ease.
May the Real Presence of God
    be your daily experience, within your heart
    and in the world of form.
May True Joy overflow into every part of your life.

You are created in the image and likeness of God. You are both male and female.

God also is both Mother and Father, sister and brother,

daughter and son, male and female essence, and all are of the One Divine Essence that is the Allness of God.

The Mother Principle is known and honored throughout the world. Only in a misunderstanding of the words of your Bible did you allow a misconception to develop of the Nature of God. God is All in All. Each of you holds the template of that Allness—the fullness of God.

It is human beings who have put interpretation on words that led many into error. And still the Mother Principle is honored in Christian countries. Even when not recognized as a part of God, you honor your mothers on Mother's Day.

Ask that any error in your understanding be healed. Ask God to clearly make Truth known to you, both in your heart and as a reflection in your world.

In the meantime, I remain your Mother. I hold you ever precious and perfect in my heart.

To be whole within yourself, you must know and honor your mother and your father—the Feminine and Masculine Principle. In honoring your earthly mother, you honor the Divine Mother. In honoring your earthly father, you honor your Heavenly Father. Only when the male and female principles are held in a position of honor and respect can you ever be whole and healed in yourself. In knowing this Essence, you come to know that Presence as part of who you really are. You learn that we are One.

You join with Jesus and say,

"I and the Father are One. I and the Mother are One."

The highest lesson of Love is that we are all One. We pray, each in our own individuality and uniqueness, to know the grace and the glory of the fulfillment of that knowledge.

I Am Mother Mary
Mother of the Cosmic Christ.

Glossary

11:11 - Symbol said to be embedded in human consciousness which was activated by certain cosmic triggers and linked to the opening of certain stargates in order to facilitate Earth's transformation at this time. Particularly associated with the work of Solara and the principle date of 1-11-1992. Many Lightworkers came together for ceremonial attunements at that time around the planet. Celebrated annually through 1999.

12-21-2012 Date in the Mayan calendar which marks the end of one cycle or age and the beginning of another. Opening of another stargate and download of cosmic energies onto the planet. This marks the entry into a transition period of five to seven years as we enter Earth's new Golden Age. Also linked to 12-12-2012 which is the same numerologically. From 12-12 to 12-21-2012 was considered a cosmic gateway.

Ascension - The specific Initiation in which one is raised in consciousness into union with the I AM Presence. There are levels upon levels of Ascension into greater and greater union with the the individuality of God called I AM.

Avatar - A Divine Being incarnated on a planet for certain vast Cosmic purposes. Krishna and Rama were considered Avatars. They were incarnations of Lord Vishnu, Sustainer of Creation. Some believe that Krishna is the Supreme Personality of Godhead and thus not an incarnation of any other Being.

Aura - The energy field of the body which includes layers reflecting the attunement with different dimensional realities. The higher realities are more subtle and extend further out, but also fully penetrate all the other, denser dimensions

.**Chakra** - An energy center. From the Sanskrit word for wheel. Traditionally, there are seven chakras identified going up the midline of the body. Each serves a specific purpose. Many now understand that there are new chakras relating to the higher frequency rays anchoring in the body. These new chakras are between the major seven.

Harmonic Convergence - August 16-17, 1987 This date was identified by José Arguelles based on study of the Mayan calendar. It is considered to be one of the first and highly significant dates which heralded the New Age and represented a time period when the first of successive waves of light reached the Earth from distant parts of the Universe, triggering planetary awakening and transformation.

Higher Self - That aspect of you which resides in the higher (heavenly) realms. Contact with the Higher Self offers truth, guidance, healing, joy, love, and spiritual replenishment. At this time, aspects of the Higher Self are merging with the human personal self in the glorious expression of the Divine Plan. This means that a new level of the Higher Self takes over the role of overseeing one's spiritual progress and development.

I AM Presence - That aspect of the Higher Self which represents the level beyond the Christ Self. The individual Divine Self which is always in union with God/Goddess/All That Is. Thus when Jesus, said, "I and the Father are One". He reflected his union on this level.

Initiation - A spiritual step which enables one to achieve a new level of consciousness, open to greater levels of love and wisdom and vibrate at a higher vibratory rate. One step of this path includes the Ascension or direct union with the I Am Presence.

Lord Jesus the Cosmic Christ - Beloved Jesus incarnated on Earth and expressed a level of Divinity that we still do not fully understand. What we can say with assurance is that the beauty of this soul and the gift that He has given us on Earth is beyond measure. We ask that you not attempt to place this being in any kind of a limited concept of who He is. Let it be to you that He is the embodiment of Love and He shares that freely with all who come to Him. (*What I can say with certainty is that He exists on every level of consciousness that I have explored to date MC*).

Logos - The Divine Being that ensouls a planet, solar system, galaxy or universe. That is, all beings within or upon a planet, etc. are part of the body and consciousness of this being.

A Planetary Logos is the Divine consciousness within which all life, in all dimensional realities, exists upon a plan-

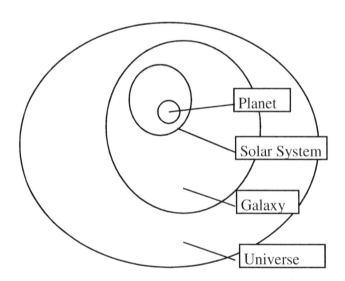

Figure G-1: Schematic representation of relationship of Planetary, Solar, Galactic and Universal Logoi.

et. A Solar Logos is the Divine consciousness which ensouls all life in a solar system. That includes the Planetary Logoi (plural) of all the planets in the system. A Galactic Logos is the Divine consciousness that ensouls all life in the galaxy including the Solar Logoi of all solar systems and the Planetary Logoi of all their planets and all beings on all dimensional levels, and so on. It is not clear to me how many levels are included in this system. More than has been described you may be sure.

Consider the esoteric meaning of the words of John as he began his gospel, "In the beginning was the word and the word was with God and the word was God . . ." Word in Greek is Logos.

(If you spend any time thinking about this system, you might notice that on Earth we have beings from all levels of consciousness. So, for example, there is an incarnation (or several) of several Galactic Logoi and the Universal Logos here on Earth. This means that those consciousnesses which hold the Logos of the Earth within themselves are themselves held within the consciousness of the Planetary Logos. So, there is a fair amount of complexity in the system.

It further means that in order for any being to come into incarnation on Earth, it must first come through the consciousness of the Universal Logos, the Galactic Logos, the Solar Logos and finally the Planetary Logos. In so doing, there is taken on the responsibility for dealing with certain lessons, issues or karma at these levels. There is much to consider in these thoughts.

(Figure G-1 looks remarkably like a cell, which can lead to some interesting thoughts, too.)

Sananda - The name that has been identified by many Lightworkers as the oversoul name for Jesus Christ. That is, Jesus was an incarnation, or one lifetime, of His Divine Self whose name is Sananda. They are fully unified—hence no separation is experienced by them. You might think of Jesus as both within this Sananda Consciousness and also fully expressing and present in levels beyond it. Sananda as a great cosmic being incarnates on various worlds as planetary messiah bringing new teachings of Love to those beings.

Sunanda - This name was revealed to Mikaelah as the Higher Self of Sananda. (Both names are mentioned as having been present during during the Krishna incarnation.) Again let us reiterate that all are of the One. Ideas that create a sense of separation are not in alignment with these beings. See this as part of the Christ that is working at very expanded levels for a specific purpose.

Yuga: - Any of four ages or eras of the world according to the Vedas, sacred Hindu texts. Each successive period is shorter, darker and less righteous than the preceding. We are presently completing the Kali Yuga—the shortest and the darkest age.

For more understanding of the complexity of these concepts I refer you to the works of Alice Bailey and to a wonderful text called "Gnosis and the Law," which represents the compiled, organized, annotated channeled information from over 30 years (1936-1972) of the top channels of the time. This material is considered the jewel teachings given to Humanity by the Spiritual Hierarchy from several publications especially the material published in the "Bridge to Freedom" series. It is not comprehensive, but contains more information about the less well known Masters and the more esoteric subjects, as well as other less well known subjects and topics, than any other source of which I am aware.

Bibliography

11:11, Solara, Star-Borne Unlimited, Whitefish, MT, 1992.

A Course in Miracles, Foundation for Inner Peace, Tiburon, CA, 1975, 1992, 1999.

The Blessed Mother's Blue Rose of the Healing Heart, Mary-Ma McChrist, The Mother Matrix, Mount Shasta, CA 1992, 1993, 1996, 1997, 1999, 2001, 2003.

Conversations with God, Neale Donald Walsch, G.P. Putnam Sons, New York, NY, 1995.

Don't Touch My Heart: Healing the Pain of an Unattached Child, Lynda Gianforte Mansfield and Christopher H. Waldmann, 1994

Phoenix Rising, Mary Summer Rain, Hampton Roads Pubishing, Charlottesville, VA, 1987

Gnosis and the Law, Tellis Papastavro, 1972 Republished by New Age Study of Humanity's Purpose, Tucson, AZ, 1980.

Initiation, Elizabeth Haich, Seed Center, Garberville, CA,1974.

Initiations, Human and Solar, Alice Bailey, Lucis Trust, New York, NY, 1933.

The Pleiadian Workbook - Awakening Your Divine Ka, Amorah Quan Yin, *Bear & Company, Santa Fe, NM, 1996.*

Take Charge of Your Life, New Age Study of Humanity's Purpose, Tucson, AZ, Vol. 9:9-10.

Products and Services

We invite you to visit our website - **www.mcordeo.4t.com** for more information about products, services and new books and e-books coming in 2013.

Treasures of Mount Shasta

DVD versions of the programs from *Treasures of Mount Shasta* TV show will be available by Spring, 2013. Check the website www.mcordeo.4t.com for more information. For questions regarding content of the television broadcasts or on your spiritual journey, Email: mcordeo1 @gmail.com

Heart of the Goddess Aromatherapy

They smell Divine!

Available in many Sacred Blends including: Buddha Mind, Christ Light, Divine Mother, Great Central Sun, I Am Presence, Goddess Quan Yin, Angel of Miracles, Angels of Healing, Guardian Angel, Love's Promise, Money, Manifesting, and Violet Flame. 4 oz. sprays in a cobalt blue glass bottle with sacred image and prayer are $16.95 each plus s/h.

For inquiries about upcoming groups or workshops
or personal channeling sessions and Ascension assistance
with Mikaelah Cordeo and the Ascended Masters
call: 928-301-8705 or email: mcordeo1@gmail.com
for more information.

Mikaelah Cordeo
Golden Rose Productions
P.O. Box 810
Mount Shasta, CA 96067
928-301-8705

ORDER FORM

Name_____

Addresss_____

City_____State____Zip_____

Country_____

Phone_____

Email_____

Credit Card # _____

Exp. Date _____ Bill me by PayPal_____
You can pay by PayPal if you prefer
Or check enclosed _____

Aromatherapy

  #   Product name $

_____ _____ _____

_____ _____ _____

_____ _____ _____

_____ _____ _____

_____ _____ _____

Books and DVDs

  #

_____ *Live in Love* _____

_____ *Gift of the Leprechauns* _____

_____ *Treasures of Mount Shasta* _____

       Dates_____

_____

       Subtotal _____

       Shipping _____

       Tax _____

       Total _____

Dear Readers,

As I worked on this next printing, I've added a few more details since we have just completed the much awaited 12-21-2012. There were many people who travelled to Mount Shasta to experience this moment here and many gatherings to honor and celebrate this moment out of time.

The coming time of transition until about 2017 is a time of consolidating our gains and expanding beyond the familiar into the time of majesty and miracles.

I am not yet ready to write a sequel to this book, but I am so grateful to those of you who have given me so much encouragement and gratitude for the blessings you have found in it. I'd like to encourage you to write or email me (mcordeo1@gmail.com) if you have further questions. I am being inspired to offer more classes and workshops on the material and as well to begin a blog which will allow you to access a variety of other information on these times.

You may go to my current website to find the link for the new blog on Earth Changes and more. www.mcordeo.4t.com.

I bless you all for your faithful work and the way that together we have healed and blessed and co-created this miracle of transformation to date and all that is to come as well.

On August 17-19, 2012, the 25th anniversary of the Harmonic Convergence, we offered *Harmonic Ascension 2012*. It was successful beyond our greatest hopes. We intend to continue to offer this event each year during this time of transition. Visit www.harmonicascension2012.com to learn more about Ascension and to sign up for current updates.

In God's Grace, may you all achieve your highest and boldest dreams. Much love to you all.

I Am Mikaelah Cordeo   12-27-2012

Printed in Great Britain
by Amazon